Hidden Gems
of
TYNESIDE

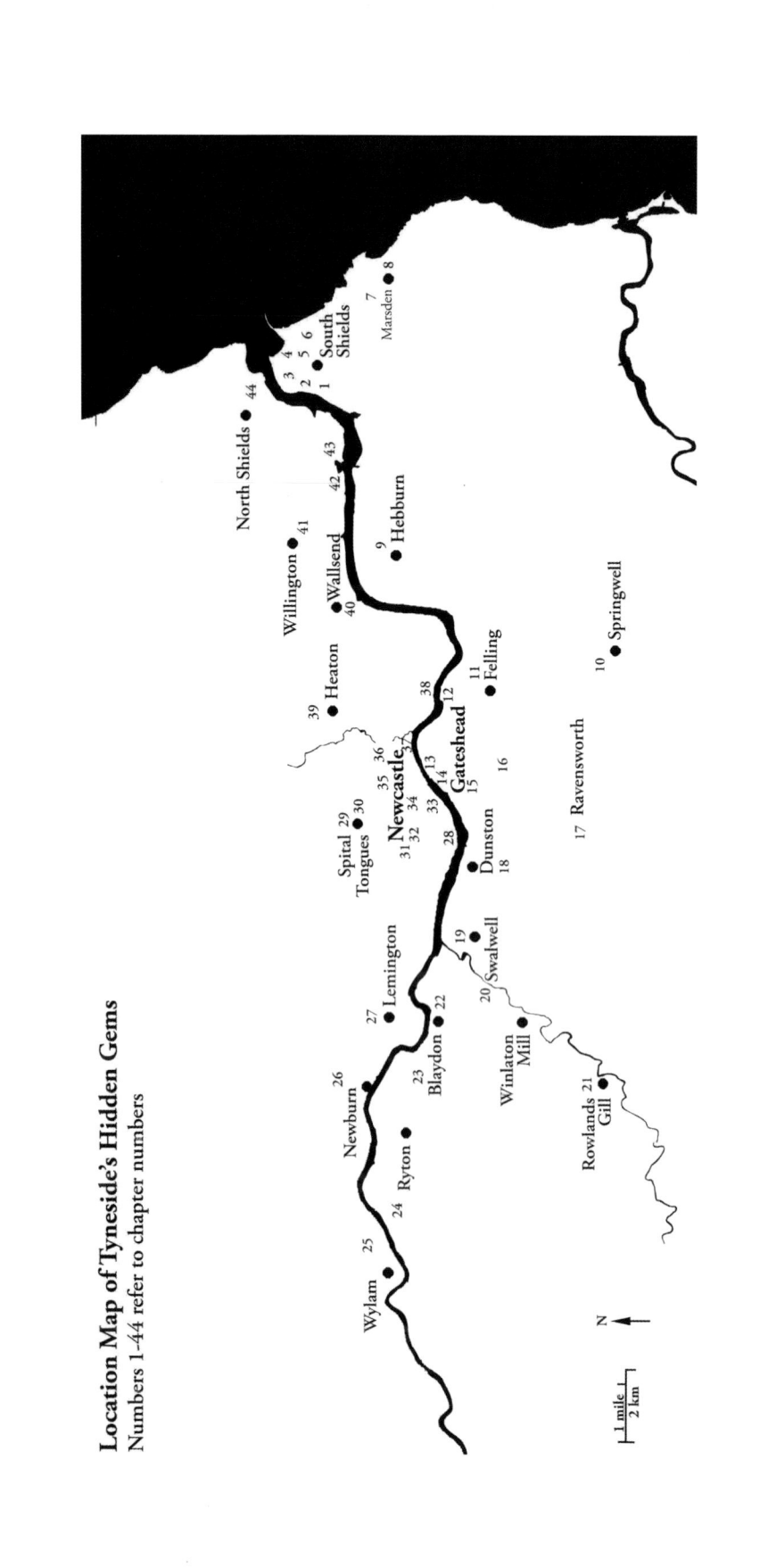

Location Map of Tyneside's Hidden Gems
Numbers 1–44 refer to chapter numbers

Hidden Gems *of* TYNESIDE

Derek Dodds

Silver Link Publishing Ltd

© Derek Dodds 2012

All rights reserved. No part of this publication may be reproduced, stored in a retrieval system or transmitted, in any form or by any means, electronic, mechanical, photocopying, recording or otherwise, without prior permission in writing from Silver Link Publishing Ltd.

First published in 2012

British Library Cataloguing in Publication Data
A catalogue record for this book is available from the British Library.

ISBN 978 1 85794 386 3

Silver Link Publishing Ltd
The Trundle
Ringstead Road
Great Addington
Kettering
Northants NN14 4BW

Tel/Fax: 01536 330588
email: sales@nostalgiacollection.com
Website: www.nostalgiacollection.com

Printed and bound in the Czech Republic

Photographs were taken by the author unless otherwise credited.

Acknowledgements

Production of this book would have been impossible without the assistance of the Local Studies staff at South Shields, Gateshead, Newcastle and North Shields Central Libraries. Anthea Lang, Gateshead's former Local History and Heritage Manager, kindly read the manuscript and suggested several improvements. Many thanks also to Hebburn historians Norman Dunn and Kevin Blair, as well as John Hayton for his insight on Newburn Almshouses. My son Andrew drew the map and sketch, and provided his usual 'technical support'. Information was generously provided by Julie Sykes from 'Go North East', the Newburn Motor Museum, and Ann and Trevor Hines of the North East Bus Preservation Trust. I must also commend the staff at Path Head Watermill for their interest and enthusiasm, and thank Mr Snowdon Oates, who permitted me to photograph Ravensworth Castle. And last, but never least, I am again indebted to John Wilks, retired curator at Tyne & Wear Museums. Once more he patiently waded through an unedited text and rescued it from various literary and historical blunders. Any that remain are entirely my responsibility.

Industry and housing developed side by side on Tyneside. Pictured in about 1925, these Lemington houses (see also page 89) seem to extend into the glassworks itself. On a bright and apparently pollution-free day, people linger in front of Cross Row. But in attempting to alleviate the general 'smoke and smells' of the glass-making process, the house-builders plunged the community into darkness – house walls facing the glassworks were windowless.
Newcastle City Library

Contents

Preface	5	
Introduction	6	
1 South Shields: a quartet of gems	11	
i St Hilda's pit		
ii Mill Dam glassworks		
iii The Alum House		
iv Market Dock		
2 South Shields: two Town Halls	18	
3 Westoe village	23	
4 Cleadon Water Tower	25	
5 Marsden: lime kilns and Souter Point	27	
6 Hebburn: St Andrew's and Hebburn Hall	33	
7 Springwell village: Bowes Railway	39	
8 Felling: Brandling Junction station	42	
9 Friar's Goose engine house	45	
10 Gateshead: Central Hotel and Greenesfield Works	47	
11 Gateshead: statue of George Hawks	50	
12 St Cuthbert's church, Bensham	52	
13 'Underhill', Kells Lane, Low Fell	55	
14 Ravensworth Castle	58	
15 Dunston Staiths	60	
16 Swalwell ironworks	63	
17 Axwell Park and Hall	68	
18 Whinfield coke works, Rowlands Gill	70	
19 Blaydon: statue of Thomas Ramsey	74	
20 Blaydon: Path Head watermill	76	
21 Clara Vale	78	
22 Wylam Waggonway	82	
23 Newburn Almshouses	85	
24 Lemington glass cone	88	
25 Elswick leadworks	90	
26 Victoria Tunnel, Newcastle	92	
27 Windmill at Chimney Mill	95	
28 South Street Locomotive Works, Newcastle	98	
29 Hanover Street, Newcastle	101	
30 Newcastle Swing Bridge	105	
31 Newcastle Brewery	110	
32 New Bridge Street, Newcastle: Dobson's House and the Lying-in Hospital	115	
33 Carliol House, Newcastle	118	
34 Keelman's Hospital, Newcastle	120	
35 Ouseburn: the Maling Pottery	123	
36 Wills cigarette factory, Heaton	126	
37 Wallsend Colliery	128	
38 Willington Ropery	131	
39 Howdon Pedestrian Tunnel	135	
40 North Shields: Albert Edward Dock	137	
41 North Shields: Maritime Chambers	140	
Index	144	

Preface

Tyneside means much more than a riverside conurbation to the almost a million people who live and work there. A high proportion of them are gathered into an almost seamless band of towns that stretch down each side of the river from Newcastle, Tyneside's capital and anchor point. Gregarious and proud though they generally are, Tynesiders are also known to relish a good argument; but whatever their individual differences or wherever their different locations, they are tied in affection to their collective 'Geordie' home. Opinions are similarly varied concerning the derivation of this historic term. It may date back to Jacobite times, when the garrison of Newcastle held firm to the Hanoverian King George; or a century later in tribute to George Stephenson, the forthright Tyneside engineer. But no matter where its origins may lie, Tyneside is as distinctive a place as the unmistakable 'Geordie' dialect that enlivens its streets.

Such streets and towns with their fascinating and historic architectural 'gems', their buildings, bridges, stately homes, statues and pubs, have helped to establish this strong sense of place, and some of them are the subject of this book. It cannot provide an exhaustive gazetteer nor be a comprehensive history. That will be found in far more detailed and scholarly works than this. Nevertheless, using archive and contemporary photographs as its subject, it embarks on an impressionistic journey around Tyneside and across this Geordie homeland. Moving westwards from the river mouth and for the most part staying close to the river shore – the region's essence – it illustrates a post-industrial landscape of profound change. It shows a landscape once inhabited by people who probably could not imagine it would ever change, a landscape that many of the latest generation can hardly imagine ever existed at all.

Now the 'coaly' Tyne runs clean and heavy industry is all but gone, yet Tyneside's gems gleam on, marking the passage of a disappearing age as well as progress into a future one. It may certainly have lost an age of great industry and invention, which caused upheaval and hardship too, but it was also an age that shaped the Tyneside of today.

Choosing the structures and locations featured here has been an unavoidably subjective process. After all, to paraphrase the recent critical comments of a regal observer, one man's gem may be another's 'monstrous carbuncle', but all of these objects, regardless of their wildly variable aesthetic qualities, can bear witness to an eventful history that created them.

Some of them are well known, even iconic perhaps, others much less so. They include uncompromising industrial marvels and celebrations of civic prosperity, scrubbed of their soot to face the modern age but still prominent landmarks in town and cityscape. Many more are harder to find, tucked shyly away down side streets or obscure and unrecognised in semi-rural backwaters. These are the true 'hidden gems', often chance survivals, their weighty significance forgotten or downplayed. Yet it is to be hoped that every one, whether they are considered to be pretentious or humble, eye-catcher or eyesore, will be sought out and enjoyed, and will grace the landscape of Tyneside for many generations to come.

Introduction
Tyneside: 'One Vast Workshop' (R. J. Charleton, 1883)

Long before the intervention of Rome and the beginning of the area's recorded history, the River Tyne may have been a tribal boundary and trading channel. Certainly the Romans swiftly recognised the strategic and economic value of this great northern river, which although difficult to navigate, particularly at its treacherous harbour mouth, had a lengthy tidal reach. The Romans built the first substantial bridges over the Tyne, at Newcastle, Corbridge and Chesters, and South Shields was established as an anchorage and supply base for the maintenance of their northern frontier. But it was not until the late medieval period that Tyneside began its rise to industrial power.

Stirrings of development were apparent by the end of the 13th century when Tyneside's wharves were a leading exporter of wool, grindstones and animal hides, and many of Newcastle's early trade guilds were associated with leather crafts. Such early trading progress must have been influenced by a maritime prowess that some contend had Viking roots, and undoubtedly over the next few centuries shipbuilding became an acknowledged Tyneside skill. Daniel Defoe singled out its importance on his journeys around the British Isles at the beginning of the 18th century. Tyneside's ships were 'built to perfection', but he could also not fail to notice the riverside glass and metal works, smoke from the saltpans at South Shields and keel men ferrying their cargoes between the shore and London-bound ships. All were dependent on coal, and it was coal that above

Introduction

all eventually transformed Tyneside into an industrial giant.

Tyneside was literally built upon coal, sitting astride rich and wide-ranging coal measures that, though not the largest in the British Isles, were for centuries the most important and became celebrated as the 'Great Northern Coalfield'. Coal had been used locally since antiquity, but it was not widely favoured until timber became scarcer during medieval times. As London's demand for household coal grew, in particular from the highly prized Tyneside High Main seam, waterborne trade flourished. At that time the advantages of river transport far outweighed notoriously unreliable roads, and by the end of the 16th century collier-borne coal exports to the capital and other European customers had increased to approximately 165,000 tons.

Following the dissolution of the monasteries, formerly church-held pits on both banks of the Tyne were leased to Newcastle merchants – the Company of Hostmen – who had long been denied the privilege and were keen to profit from the demand for Tyneside's 'seacole' during Elizabethan times. But as some of the shallower, more accessible riverside seams were exhausted, ways had to be found to transport coal to the river from further inland. Coal and its profitability was a catalyst for change. It had originally been hauled along often impassable paths between pithead and staith by packhorse, cart and wagon. But after an initial introduction of a waggonway in Nottinghamshire and a partially successful attempt at Blyth by Huntingdon Beaumont, what was probably the Tyne's first waggonway opened in 1621. 'Chaldrons', wooden carts carrying up to 3 tons of coal, rattled the few miles between Whickham and Dunston, and Britain's age of rail was under way. Wherever practical, bridges, cuttings and embankments were constructed to aid the waggoner and his horse. At the chaldron's destination, impressive riverside staiths were erected, using spouts to funnel coal directly on to the decks of the waiting flat-bottomed keelboats. Within a century Tyneside was laced with waggonway routes, some of which were pathfinders for a future railway network. Britain was on the cusp of an industrial revolution, which Tyneside was well-positioned to later exploit.

As the pulse of Tyneside's industrial economy quickened, wooden rails were replaced with iron and horsepower was largely replaced by metal and steam. But coal was vital for the production of both. Organised metalworking came to the North East towards the end of the 17th century. The ready availability of cheap fuel for his ironmongery processes drew Midlands ironmaster Ambrose Crowley to Winlaton in 1691, where he established a nail-making factory regulated by manufacturing principles that were subsequently widely adopted. Chains and anchors to fulfil Admiralty contracts also flowed from his works, encouraging local entrepreneurs to follow his example and rival his success. Most notable among these was William Hawks, a

This photograph from about 1920 shows miners, safety lamps lit, preparing to descend Redheugh pit in Gateshead.

former employee of Crowley, who opened his Gateshead premises in 1747, forging billets from the iron waste carried back to the Tyne as ballast by the collier fleet. Employees of both companies, 'Crowley's Crew' and 'Haaks Men', competed for work and famously fought each other on local streets. Commercially at least, Hawks and his dynasty certainly eclipsed the Crowley empire, but steam power in the bulky shape of a 12-horsepower Boulton & Watt engine also played a crucial role in the Gateshead man's ultimate success.

Tyneside grasped at the improvements made in steam engine technology during the 18th century and became a test-bed for their introduction and development. The Newcomen pumping engine, first introduced into tin mines by their inventor, was relatively crude and inefficient, but was initially also a Cornish-sent solution to the problem of Tyneside's flooded mine galleries. Its heavy fuel consumption was largely irrelevant in the northern coalfield where by mid-century hundreds of them puffed and snorted away at their work. Formerly unreachable coal reserves were now available and Tyneside took an economic step forward. Almost half of all British coal production in 1815 began its journey from north-eastern pits. No doubt Watt's further steam power improvements were indispensable to this, but his revolutionary machines, now capable of pumping, winding and a score of other industrial applications, were just as dependent on a reliable source of cheap fuel. And as well as Hawks, other Tyneside men were also impressed and inspired by these technological advances. William Hedley and Timothy Hackworth became pioneers in railway technology, but it was their contemporary, George Stephenson, who is remembered – not quite deservedly perhaps – as the 'Father of the Railways'. Yet undoubtedly it was the Stephenson family, together with architects and builders Dobson and Grainger, who worked to change the 'coaly' face of Tyneside.

And where small coals were plentiful,

Tyneside's engineering skills: a ship's main gear wheel, circa 1946.

chemical production was never far away. Traditional salt production on the riverside became more sophisticated as populations grew and their everyday requirements increased. Demand for alkali, the mainstay of products such as soap, glass and bleaching agents, led to Britain's first adoption of the groundbreaking Leblanc process on Tyneside. This French discovery enabled soda to be produced from salt and sulphuric acid, paving the way for mass-production of an indispensable chemical ingredient. Local chemist and coal-owner William Losh opened his alkali plant at Walker on the outskirts of Newcastle in 1791. Over the next decades its lofty chimneys were followed by a forest of others, adding to the pall of acrid chemical fumes that were infamous characteristics of a polluted Victorian Tyneside. Nevertheless, as the young Queen Victoria began her long reign, Tyneside

Introduction

possessed the ample raw materials, human skills and ingenuity to benefit from the coming acceleration of industrialisation.

If Tyneside was renowned for coal, rail and iron innovation, it will also be remembered for its ships, the famous names of so many of which tripped off local tongues as readily as they rolled down the slipways. For all of them, whether ocean liner, powerful warship or tramp steamer, their greatest accolade was to be classified as 'Tynebuilt', a watchword for seaworthiness achieved through long-practised engineering excellence.

Shipwrights were busy on the river for centuries, especially it appears around the Ouseburn inlet, not far from Newcastle's medieval walls. But it was not until the 19th century that the twisting and turning Tyne, which had slowed commercial progress and was likened by frustrated early navigators to a 'River Dragon', began to be tamed. *Vulcan*, a rowing boat launched in 1822, was reputedly the Tyne's first iron vessel, and less than two decades later the region's first iron steamer set sail from a South Shields yard. Tyneside's waterborne revolution was at last under way, harnessing steam and iron to ships and attracting pioneers to design and oversee their construction. Just like their ships and allied enterprises, the names of many of these maritime trailblazers are justifiably well known. Armstrong, Mitchell and Palmer, for example, were giants in the field, but many more, in their own way equally clever and resourceful, quietly plied their trade in smaller operations along the river's length. Their blend of practicality and business acumen helped to foster an industry that led the world. At its finest hour, in 1907, one Tyneside yard alone produced 15 per cent of the world's total shipping tonnage. Writing of the great pre-war years, when the British Empire and Tyneside reached their peak, Newcastle historian R. J. Charleton vividly evokes the clamour and activity of bustling industry. Tyneside was an industrial cauldron and had indeed become 'one vast workshop'. It was a workshop that supplied the world – a closely integrated mesh of manufacturing that had created Tyneside's power, but which was also to become its Achilles heel.

However, without the craft and labour of countless Tynesiders, none of this could have been achieved. These anonymous people hewed the coal, forged the metal, built the engines, launched the ships and worked in the host of ancillary and interdependent industries on which the area increasingly relied.

The forebears of many modern Tynesiders were work-hungry immigrants, attracted to the magnet of Tyneside, particularly from Scotland and Ireland during the 19th and early 20th century. They found a Tyneside that, apart from the growing sprawl of its capital Newcastle, was dotted along the river shore. Small communities were gathered haphazardly around their parish church or pit shaft, within easy reach of shipyards or chemical works. Hamlets became towns as the terraced rows stretched back from the river, and urban Tyneside, with its new churches, municipal parks, monuments and civic buildings, began to take shape. Between 1801 and the turn of the following century the population of Northumberland and Durham quadrupled to create what has been described as a 'social melting pot'. Great commercial expansion in Tyneside was a major contribution to this, but it also produced a prosperity never shared by all. Industrial wages were generally higher but the effort to earn them was just as demanding and even more dangerous than agricultural toil. Funeral bells tolled long and frequently across Tyneside, marking not just mass fatalities in its gas-laden pits, but the insidious loss of life above ground in manufacturing and other lethal industrial processes.

Thus life for the majority at this time was punctuated by extreme uncertainty. But it also showed that wildly fluctuating economies are not confined to the vagaries of modern markets alone. During the relatively successful Victorian era enterprises still failed and demand often plummeted, at times forcing Tyneside's workers to become wanderers once more. Depressions were severe, though often short-lived, and Tyneside was no stranger to poverty, squalor and despair. The four decades that straddle the 19th and 20th centuries are regarded as a 'boom' time for local trade and industry. The world had beaten a path to Tyneside for coal and chemicals, ships, armaments and manufactured goods. But no one was prepared for the 'bust' to come.

Like props supporting a heavy mine roof, the industrial underpinnings of Tyneside's economy began to be knocked away. Even before the 1930s slump the local chemical industry had begun to suffer. Tyneside was overtaken by Teesside and the Mersey, and in 1900 only four heavy chemical works remained from an industry that once employed more than 10,000. 'King Coal' also began to falter. It was not a sudden collapse but a stuttering decline in the years after the First World War. As a consequence of the Treaty of Versailles, coal exports – the lifeblood of Tyneside – were seriously curtailed and associated industries suffered accordingly.

Yet all was not gloom. Work went on and the area was never to become the industrial desert it is sometimes portrayed. For example, although sometimes underestimated, Tyneside's electrical industry was an employment lifeline to the area throughout the 20th century. However, a combination of competition, technological change and a peculiarly British brand of industrial conflict helped to lose Tyneside's industrial crown. By the opening of the new millennium Tyneside had closed its last deep pit, shipbuilding was coming to an end and the landscape was being transformed. Coal tips became country parks, factories were turned to superstores and neat industrial estates were laid out on derelict industrial sites.

But Tyneside has endured with enough resilience to take on the testing challenges to come. From the melting pot emerged strong communities welded together by their history of shared hardships. Though massive social change and industrial upheaval subsequently broke many of them apart, their spirit somehow survived. Today most Tynesiders lay fierce claim to a cultural and regional identity all their own, a passion firmly anchored in a distinctive if sometimes vaguely understood past. Today's browsing city centre shoppers or Quayside revellers may be largely oblivious of the industrial history that surrounds them, but it is a distinctive and remarkable history, some of which may hopefully shine out from the following pages.

Three miles north of Newcastle, now incongruous among bungalows and blocks of flats, stands the 'Main Dike Stone'. Erected in 1828, it marked the overcoming of the Ninety Fathom Dike – a geological disturbance that had blocked access to rich coal reserves. It was a significant moment for the opening of Gosforth Colliery (which was celebrated with a subterranean ball attended by more than 200 people) and a milestone for the subsequent development of the Great Northern Coalfield. A similar stone lies not far away in the churchyard of Gosforth's parish church.

1. South Shields: a quartet of gems
i. St Hilda's pit

From the edge of the market place to the harbour mouth is a bracing walk along the waterfront and through the history of South Shields. Once a claustrophobic tangle of heavy manufacturing and workers' accommodation, the area has become a haven for shopping, entertainment and smart riverside living. But half-forgotten and often unremarked among the new, four rare gems of Shields's old industry survive.

On a slope above the market place, but now concealed amongst the latest 'retail developments', are the last vestiges of this seaside town's considerable mining heritage. Named after the adjacent parish church, the Hilda colliery began to win coal in 1825, three years after being opened by Newcastle coal and railway entrepreneurs Robert and John Brandling. Shields's first pit at nearby Templetown had proved too costly

St Hilda's pit is pictured here during its final years in the 1950s. Site clearance has begun and a controlled explosion in 1954 demolished the colliery yard's landmark chimney. *South Tyneside Libraries (South Shields)*

Modern Shields now draws closer to the last remnants of St Hilda's. Its headstocks and early 20th-century pumping house were conserved as a mark of respect for those killed in the 1839 explosion. It was a tragic day for South Shields but it led eventually to safety improvements in British pits.

to operate, and the new workings similarly battled against the perils of flooding and gas. Nevertheless, St Hilda's produced enough coal to provide a living for many Shields townspeople in the turbulent century to come.

But it was hard-won coal in every respect. Although about 50,000 tons of coal per year was exported in the 1830s, the men who cut it were also embroiled in the intense political conflict of the day. Their infant trade union fought to improve pay and conditions, and soldiers were garrisoned in the town after an outbreak of riots against the 'Bond', the resented yearly contract that tied miners to individual collieries. But when their protest failed and work resumed, St Hilda's pit proved to be as uncompromising as its owners. The greatest tragedy was in June 1839, when 51 men and boys died as a consequence of a huge explosion.

However, the underground gloom was sometimes penetrated by invention and hope. Hilda pit had been an early testing ground for the use of metal shaft linings. Similarly, in the aftermath of the disaster, a local committee made farsighted recommendations on improvements to mine ventilation. One of its members in particular, James Mather, was commended for his major contribution to miners' welfare when he gave evidence to a later parliamentary inquiry. Mather – writer, reformer, inventor and tireless anti-slavery campaigner – took part in rescue attempts in 1839 and is certainly one of Tyneside's unsung heroes. In South Shields he is commemorated only by a street name.

By the early years of the Second World War, coal production from Hilda pit was effectively ended. It had been gradually superseded by newer workings at Harton, Whitburn and Westoe, and though enjoying a brief post-war revival, the pit ended its days as a ventilation and escape shaft for one of these neighbouring mines. An uncertain future for its redundant pumping house was only resolved by the granting of listed status and renovation in 2000. Visually unappealing it may be, but this chunk of history is an undeniable gem. It serves to remind us of a history fuelled by coal, the 'black diamonds' of Shields and all industrial Tyneside.

ii. Mill Dam glassworks

Passers-by occasionally stop and wonder at the entrance to the picturesque Mill Dam in South Shields. On the right, beyond the cobbled street, is a squat brick pillar bearing a date plaque of 1865.

Introduction: South Shields: a quartet of gems

Some speculate that it was a navigation beacon for the river channel that once teemed with ships, but more mundanely perhaps it is in fact a truncated chimney from a former glassworking site.

Glass manufacturing was established in Shields by Newcastle merchant Isaac Cookson in the middle of the 17th century. After the Civil War, Newcastle's long-held grip on river trade was loosened and the Cookson family seem to have seized the opportunity to establish a string of businesses around South Shields. Glassmaking became one of their largest and most successful ventures; raw materials were ferried in and domestic glass was shipped out from their factory wharf, which was long remembered as 'Cookson's Quay'. It is believed that local glassblowers, whose strength and skill fashioned the primitive blooms into shape, produced Britain's first window plate glass in the Cookson works.

Over time this relatively crude early craft became a significant manufacturing process, but with the growing demand for glass the Cookson operation unsurprisingly faced fierce competition. Eight large factories were at work in the town by 1827, yet Cookson's remained supreme and indeed grew stronger as, ten years later, sheet glass began to roll from the Mill Dam works. A new owner, Robert Swinburne, extended and modernised the works, which continued until bankruptcy intervened.

At the opening of the 20th century only one glass manufacturer remained in South Shields, but remarkably the Swinburne chimney hung on. Enclosed by a boiler works, rail sidings and the web of lines that carried coal to Harton Staiths, the industrial relic stood undisturbed until well into the 20th century. Shortened in 1973, it was saved from further indignity when a few years later the Mill Dam area was awarded conservation status and redeveloped into a lively arts and entertainment quarter. Although there are proposals to build around it again, the glassworks chimney for now stands alone – a last gasp of a lost industry.

Swinburne's chimney stands in the background of this view, competing for attention with the tower of the 1885 Seamen's Mission on the right. Taken in the late 1930s, the view is looking across Mill Dam to colliers lying off Harton Staiths. Once the route of an obscure creek sometimes called the Branin, the area was gradually reclaimed in the 19th century to become a hub of the town's seagoing trade. Merchant seamen often gathered here and it was the scene of an infamous riot in 1930.
South Tyneside Libraries (South Shields)

As this recent photograph shows, only the stump of the glassworks chimney is now visible, and Mill Dam's cobbled street is a car park for cinema and theatregoers at the former Customs House.

The old chimney base stands alone at present, but may soon be joined by a new business centre planned for Harton Staiths.

iii. The Alum House

Local history is often hinted at in the names of public houses, and none more so than 'The Alum Ale House', possibly South Shields's oldest

From this early 1900's photograph it is easy to appreciate how the Alum House could have been the first port of call for thirsty scullermen. These 'grizzled and weather-beaten sea dogs' piloted early South Shields ferries and some used the historic landing, which can be glimpsed at the river's edge, only yards from the pub's entrance.
South Tyneside Libraries (South Shields)

In 2010 the tradition continues. The *Pride of the Tyne* sets off from a new ferry staging in the shadow of the Alum Ale House. Completed in 1993 by Swan Hunters at Wallsend, *Pride* holds the dubious distinction of being one of the last ships to be built on the Tyne. She now also shares the Tyne's last remaining ferry service to North Shields with the *Spirit of the Tyne*, which began operating four years later.

Introduction: South Shields: a quartet of gems

riverside drinking haunt. The production of alum, a basic constituent of early glassmaking, followed hard on the heels of Shields's first glass factory. Alum shale from north of Whitby was landed on the foreshore at the 'Ham', one of the town's long-established moorings. Subsequently, the chemical works that overshadowed it became known as the 'Alum House', and an adjoining hostelry that welcomed generations of parched workers was certainly open by the mid-19th century. Like many busy seaports at that time, South Shields was well provided with taverns and pubs. The town was said to 'swarm' with them in 1834, and then as now the authorities fretted over the control of licences and the social evils of under-age drinking. More than 150 inns are recorded and their array of decorated signs must have brightened an otherwise drab environment.

Since then the Alum House pub has become a riverside gem, and over the last half-century has emerged from a warren of demolished works and tenements to be clearly visible next to Shields's latest cross-river ferry service. As well as a reputation for its wines and real ales, the pub has become well known for spirits of a more supernatural kind. Various ghostly characters from Shields's colourful past have been sighted, the most mischievous among them being deterred from causing mayhem amongst the glassware by brass rails stretching behind the bar. Regardless of this, the venerable public house has retained its popularity over the years and continues to slake the thirst of townspeople and visitors alike.

Despite recent difficulties, the Alum House keeps on trading, and its own more spectral cast of characters, including 'Giggly Meg' and the 'Phantom Barman', appear to be unmoved.

iv. Market Dock

Market Dock forms a dramatic and surprising centrepiece to one of Shields's newest riverfront housing schemes. The former Brigham & Cowan's dry dock, although in service for less than 30 years, remains a potent symbol of a much older trade. Shipbuilding and repairing commenced in the early 18th century and in 1789 was significantly advanced with the opening of Simon Temple's dry dock, reputed at the time to be among the best-equipped in Britain. While his business ventures ultimately failed, other competitors flourished and, after the difficult post-Napoleonic decades, South Shields captured a lion's share of shipbuilding on the Tyne.

The paddle steamer *Star*, launched from the lee of Shields harbour in 1839, was arguably the Tyne's first iron ship and the town entered the 20 century with shipbuilding and repairing firmly established. Industrialists Brigham and Cowan seized upon this, constructing their first large 'graving dock' or dry dock in 1905. It rubbed shoulders with much older and more seasoned firms, but Brigham's soon became a household name and a cornerstone of local employment.

Ship repairing was always a dirty and dangerous occupation, requiring a high degree of skilful improvisation. As water was pumped from the dock, the vessel settled onto keel blocks and was braced by wooden props allowing work to commence. A myriad of tasks were then carried out, from the replacement of damaged platework to the overhaul and replacement of machinery. Hulls were routinely cleaned and repainted and many jobs were done in the 'dock bottom', an uncomfortable and unpopular place. Desperate to keep their fleets trading, ship-owners often imposed tight deadlines, and while this could potentially mean better contract prices and higher wages in overtime, it also led to short-term employment and

The Sunderland-built grain carrier *Ixia*, owned by the Stag Line of North Shields, is pictured here undergoing a refit within Brigham & Cowan's new 715-foot-long dry dock. The vessel looks ready to take advantage of Brigham's improved facilities, which were said to provide everything from 'washes and brushes up to complicated ship surgery'. New workshops, seen on the right of the dock, were constructed to speed this along.
Courtesy of Norman Dunn

Artist Irene Brown's 'Fleet' now fills the dock and orderly housing has replaced the clutter of dockside paraphernalia. Once lined with the cranes of Smith's Docks, the opposite riverbank is becoming another potential building site.

increased the pressure on an already hard-pressed workforce.

Nevertheless, Brigham & Cowan's yard survived the rollercoaster of the United Kingdom's economy, and in the 1950s anticipated a period of expansion. Brigham's modern dock was opened in September 1956 to great local expectation. However, in 1982 the yard was closed, its new owner, the British Shipbuilders Corporation, unable to stem the tide of decline in national shipbuilding. Fifteen years later bulldozers moved in, but the dock was spared to become an attractive selling point for the marina-style accommodation that rose from the flattened shipyard.

Today, Brigham's last dock is well hidden by the fashionable apartments gathered around it on 'Captain's Wharf'. Seven stainless-steel sculptures of colliers, facing the former dock gates and the river beyond, are its latest occupants.

2. South Shields: two Town Halls

Civic pride is well served in South Shields. It can proudly boast of not one but two fine Town Halls. Stylistically, they differ greatly, yet each is a splendid architectural gem and both are products of important periods during the development of this historic seaside town.

Almost 1,000 years after the Romans deserted their fort overlooking the harbour, Shields emerges from history as the 'vill at Suthcheles', trading in bread, beer and fish. Salt production is later recorded and a few brine pans in use at the end of the 15th century had become 200 by 1743.

This quickening commercial pace demanded expansion of the town, which before then was crowded along the Tyne foreshore for a mile and a half, leaving little

This unusual panorama of Shields market place in the 1930s gives a largely unobstructed view of the old Town Hall. Of course this was a time of fewer traffic restrictions when private transport was more of a luxury than a necessity. The cars in the photograph are a Ford Model B saloon and, parked on the right, a Morris 10/4 with a Newcastle City registration. Some things never change, however, and in 1808 the town's magistrates were most concerned about the 'conduct of young persons' around the market place and the town hall. The fine Georgian structure narrowly escaped the worst of the Blitz in 1941 and was renovated in 1977. *South Tyneside Libraries (South Shields)*

A one-way traffic system now operates around the market place, yet surrounded by market stalls, Shields's original civic centre remains a focus of modern town life.

room for the necessary fairs and weekly markets. Subsequently, an 8-acre parcel of glebe land, adjoining the parish church of St Hilda, was acquired for the provision of a new market place and additional housing, and in about 1768 a 'quaint edifice' was built at its centre. It may have been the work of a local man and was soon popularly known as the 'cross', probably recalling a pre-existing monument. The attractive Town Hall, its arches and Tuscan columns topped by a curiously elongated 'pepper-pot' cupola, was designed with an open arcade on the ground floor. This provided for general trading in corn and provisions, allowing the enclosed area above to be used for more official town business. During the next century the homely little building was a focus for town activity and became a popular meeting place for unemployed seamen on the look-out for their next ship. But South Shields did not stand still and continued to spread out from the riverbank. During the 19th century the town's population increased tenfold, leaving little doubt that its first civic centre had been outgrown.

In 1850, following a petition listing the town's numerous successful industries, South Shields became a municipal borough. 'Always Ready' was adopted as the fledgling borough's motto by a council who were certainly ready for a new town hall to match their town's enhanced status. However, various schemes to rebuild on the same site were abandoned in the face of a public outcry against demolition of the original. The people of

Dressed in what appears to be their Sunday best, South Shields townsfolk hurry past their new Town Hall. Predating the unveiling of Queen Victoria's statue in May 1913, this image captures well the town's magnificent but much delayed municipal building. Following disputes and delays it was opened in 1910 costing a well-over-budget £78,386. Remarkably, even its completion was marred by controversy – dispute about the quality of fittings led to a bizarre 'siege' involving the contractors.
South Tyneside Libraries (South Shields)

South Shields: two Town Halls

Extended in the 1960s and its stonework cleaned of industrial grime in 1973, Shields's Town Hall can often be taken for granted. But as shown by this contemporary photo, it is now South Tyneside's pride and joy.

South Shields had taken the picturesque old building to their hearts, and it was a further half-century before the vexing subject was raised once more.

As Queen Victoria's epic reign drew to a close, plans were laid again. However, none of them now proposed the removal of the original municipal building. A new, more prominent site was eventually chosen on higher ground to the south of the town's increasingly complex grid pattern of streets. London architect Ernest Fetch was chosen to design the 'elaborate pile' required to accommodate the growing army of officials and administrators that South Shields Council now employed.

On 19 October 1910 the long-drawn-out saga ended with the opening of the new municipal buildings. Influenced by the Baroque style, they evoke days of Empire and Edwardian confidence. Britannia is enthroned on a cannon above the entrance, but high above her the town's debt to the sea is also acknowledged. A sailing ship, modelled in copper, floats on top of the lofty north-west clock tower, and acts as a weathervane for the great building.

Since it was built, the 'new' town hall has been widely admired and is often agreed to be the finest in the county. Without doubt this grand civic gem has eclipsed its diminutive forerunner, which now sits hidden in the market place, screened by bland modernity. The contrast between old and new could not be greater. One, simple and provincial, was the product of an infant community. The other, sophisticated and cosmopolitan, marks the coming of age of a thriving town.

Yet today, walking through the arcade of the first town hall into a bustling market place, it might be thought that the heart and soul of South Shields has not travelled very far.

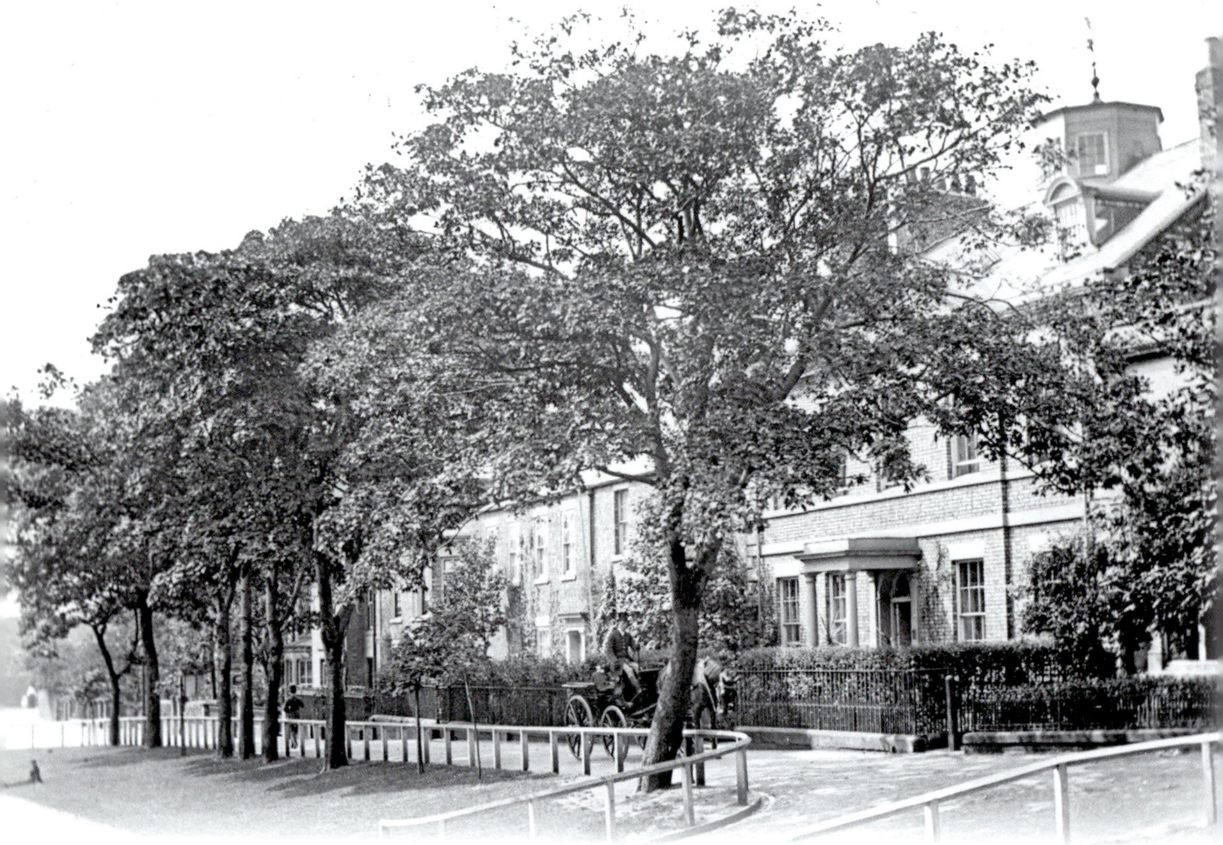

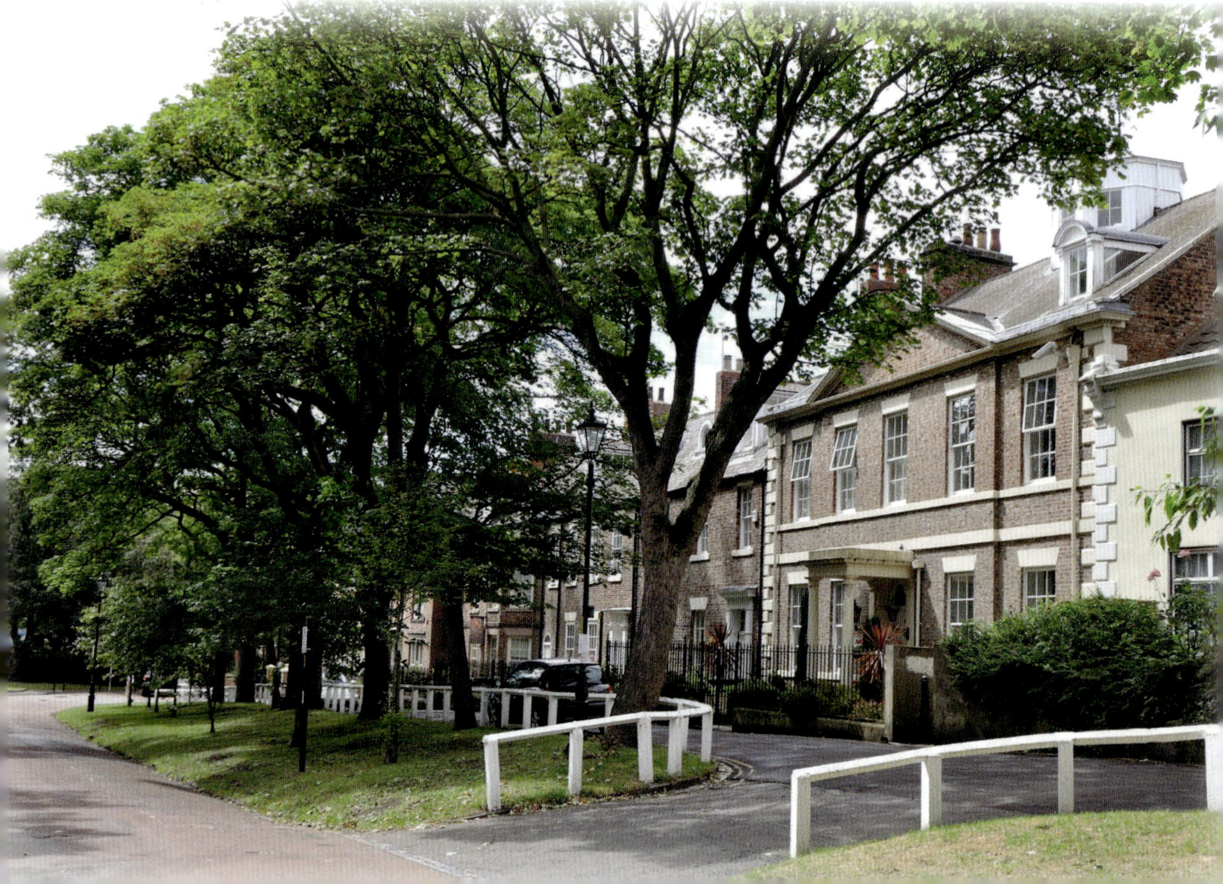

3. Westoe village

Westoe village is a well-kept secret. Hidden a few steps away from a main road and barely a mile from the centre of one of Tyneside's busiest towns is the former main street of a once tranquil and isolated medieval hamlet.

Westoe's history is as ancient as South Shields, which grew prodigiously around it. Certainly after the Norman Conquest, and probably long before, it was in ecclesiastical hands, possessing a manor house and chapel often visited by the Prior of Durham and his retinue on their stately progress around the Bishopric. At that time the boundaries of Westoe's old township stretched much further than today, encompassing marshland around Jarrow to the west and reaching the harbour mouth to the north. For centuries most of this was agricultural land, cultivated by generations of tenant farmers. In 1186, when Durham's miniature version of Domesday, the 'Boldon Buke' was compiled, Westoe was valued at 13 marks. But disease and war destroyed any further glimmers of prosperity, and by the close of the 14th century decline had set in. Farming continued, but Westoe's few substantial buildings, robbed of their dressed stones for farm and garden buildings, shrunk into the fields. Only the tower of St Lawrence's chapel could be seen in 1750, as the neighbouring town began to expand and draw nearer.

Yet ironically the development of Shields gave a new lease of life to its rural neighbour. From a slight slope, Westoe looked down towards the Tyne and the industry ranging along the river shore. Increasingly, Westoe was seen as a peaceful retreat for the local elite. Some of their fine houses have survived, often heavily altered and stylistically muddled, but 'gems' none the less.

Successful men from all walks of life purchased plots of village land, but industrialists in particular also appear have been attracted by Westoe's relative seclusion. For them it was just a short carriage ride away but a world apart from the grimy factories and shipyards where their fortunes were made. Among them were the Marshall family – ship-owners and merchants, originally from Whitby – and James Cochran Stevenson, who came to Westoe about 1857 to become the new lord of the manor.

Son of a Scottish cotton and chemical magnate, James Stevenson built his family home on the supposed site of the medieval manor, and went on to play a significant part in public life, becoming mayor and a long serving MP for South Shields. His spacious mansion, designed by his brother, was seriously damaged by fire in 1868 but was remodelled and became generally known as Westoe Hall after it was purchased by subsequent owner James Readhead in 1895. He too was a leading light in civic affairs, and his shipbuilding business was among the foremost on the Tyne, going on to launch more than 600 vessels in a long and largely prosperous history.

It is tempting to imagine these captains

A horse and carriage wait outside one of Westoe's fashionable residences in this photograph from about 1905. Prominent on the leafy avenue's north side is the Tuscan columned porch of No 8. Diagonally opposite James Readhead's Westoe Hall, this house is dated 1810, but some parts are probably older. It was home to the Marshall family, originally from Whitby, who as well as merchants and local dignitaries were described as 'large shipowners' in South Shields. *South Tyneside Libraries (South Shields)*

Apart from the inevitable parked cars, time appears to have stood still in Westoe. This area at the top of the village adjacent to Sunderland Road once contained a large pond that was drained and planted with trees after 1859. For many years in the 20th century the former Marshall house was a Tyneside branch of the Talbot House Association, better known as 'Toc H' – the community-based charitable organisation founded in 1915 by Reverend 'Tubby' Clayton.

of industry scanning the coastline and perhaps looking towards their South Shields businesses from the comfort of their rooftop belvederes. As the 20th century progressed, momentous changes could be observed from the panoramic viewpoints. The town spread out and industries rose and fell. But through it all, Westoe has stood apart. It has somehow clung on to a genteel charm, its tree-lined verges and handsome buildings a quiet haven in a restless modern world.

Built about 1864, red-bricked Westoe Hall and its glazed rooftop lantern are pictured here in September 2010.

4. Cleadon Water Tower

Soaring gracefully above Cleadon village on the outskirts of South Shields, the 'Water Tower', as it is generally known, is one of South Tyneside's more romantic industrial gems. This red-brick structure is more down-to-earth, however, having been built as a chimney to serve a 19th-century waterworks.

Clean and adequate water supplies were a major priority for the burgeoning town of South Shields during the Victorian years, particularly after a serious cholera outbreak in 1831. Around this time much of the town depended on a makeshift system of water carts, barrels and primitive storage 'pants', and industries laid their own pipes from local, often polluted sources. The neighbouring hamlet of Cleadon, on rising ground and lying over water-bearing limestone rock formations, was therefore ripe for development. Wells had long been sunk there, but with the formation of the town corporation, order and Victorian civil engineering expertise was brought to the provision of water.

The vital task was accordingly placed in the hands of the newly formed Sunderland & South Shields Water Company, which by 1863 had constructed a typically grand waterworks complex and erected the landmark 100-foot chimney that exists today.

Within a year of commissioning, the two Cornish engines at the waterworks' core were supplying a quarter of a million gallons daily, but even this was not enough. Increasing demand from local industry required the development of resources further afield, and a similar but plainer water pumping facility was constructed at Ryhope, on the outskirts of Sunderland. Consulting Engineer Thomas Hawksley designed both stations, but, unlike Ryhope, which continued until 1967

The unmistakable profile of Cleadon Water Tower counterbalances an unexploded German mine in the foreground of this wartime photograph. The aftermath of an air raid in April 1941 appears to have confirmed the fears of local inhabitants, convinced that the Luftwaffe used the chimney as a pathfinder for their attacks. Waterworks were regarded as legitimate targets by the enemy, but it is just as likely that a fire-lit decoy at nearby Wellands Farm placed Cleadon on the front line during night bombing. From 1940, devices known as 'Special Fire' or 'Starfish' sites were secretly deployed to protect Britain's industrial conurbations and in the course of the war saved many lives. South Tyneside Libraries (South Shields)

This archive photograph shows Cleadon pumping station with most of its original buildings intact. The narrowness of the site is illustrated and may explain why the 'smoke tower' or 'roving chimney', as the Water Tower is more technically described, was placed above the boiler house. An underground flue connected these structures. A large circular reservoir – later given a concrete cover – was included in the newly built complex, which was estimated to have cost about £60,000. *South Tyneside Libraries (South Shields)*

Though the town of South Shields continues to expand, Cleadon has retained a country atmosphere. High above the fields, Thomas Hawksely's gem of a chimney is a reference point for walks around the surrounding Cleadon Hills, with their ruined 19th-century windmill and spectacular coastal views.

Cleadon Water Tower

Hawksley's Tower, July 2010.

and is still in working order, nothing remains of Cleadon's original machinery.

Indeed, it is fortunate that anything of the site has survived at all. Throughout an often precarious history it has come under attack from various quarters. Doubts about the lofty chimney were forcibly expressed from the start. Although it appeared on Admiralty charts, it was feared in 1866 that the new chimney was a navigational hazard, luring ships on to treacherous cliffs nearby.

Despite this, Cleadon's decorous pumping station served the region for more than a century. Electric power came in 1931, and afterwards the redundant chimney provided a superb location for a radio station and the telecommunications aerials that still clutter the exterior brickwork. Sometimes threatened by demolition, the chimney's historical status was eventually acknowledged and, with the conversion of some station buildings to private use, the future of this fascinating monument has finally become secure.

Debate persists on the architectural merits of this ostentatious gem. Stylistically it is often compared to a pagoda or a campanile. Equally comfortable in an Oriental palace or the hills of Tuscany as it may be, Thomas Hawksley's Tower is now widely admired and comfortably at home in suburban Cleadon.

Marsden's lime kilns are pictured here as they were in 1901. Looking north towards South Shields harbour, the photograph clearly illustrates the kiln sheds and the railway system that served them – shuttling in raw materials and removing processed lime. On the embankment to the right is a 10½-ton truck, while in the middle distance projects the roof of Marsden's first public railway station. Opened in 1879 as a mineral line between Whitburn's new colliery and South Shields, the coastal rail link also provided a general passenger service after 1888. Nicknamed the 'Marsden Rattler' because of its bone-shaking ride, the line was officially closed in 1953 but was used for a last nostalgic trip in 1968. *Durham County Record Office*

Road transport now dominates the Marsden scene. Marsden station was removed in 1926 to make way for the new coast road, and the abandoned kilns are now fenced off. The original track bed in front of them is still conspicuous, together with a concrete and brick platform, added towards the end of the kiln's working life to modernise lime transportation.

5. Marsden: lime kilns and Souter Point

Sweeping views and seaside air have made the coastline at Marsden a popular local attraction. Visitors may not suspect, however, that what appears to be a pristine landscape is largely man-made. Well within living memory, what is now a cliff-top coastal park was overrun with industry and riddled with mines and quarries and their leftover spoil. Since then the tracks of Marsden's staple industries and the community that relied upon them have been well covered, but in a meadow sprinkled with wild flowers stands a monolithic bank of Victorian lime kilns. As yet avoiding 'regeneration', they are a crumbling remnant of a once important manufacturing operation.

Perhaps because it was so widespread, lime-burning appears to be the poor relation

H. C. Casserley's evocative photograph captures the 'Rattler' hard at work. NER 'C' Class locomotive No 8 steams across Lighthouse Bridge towards Whitburn Colliery station in April 1934. Marsden's lighthouse – just caught in the background – actually stands on Lizard Point, but was named Souter (which is just to the south) to avoid any confusion with the Cornish peninsula. *South Tyneside Libraries (South Shields)*

of industrial processes, attracting scant attention compared to iron-working or the winning of coal. Yet lime has always been fundamental to the production of mortar and cement, iron and chemicals, and had many other uses including soil fertilisation and the decorative waterproofing of houses. Traditionally, small temporary lime kilns were often set up on building sites or in the countryside near limestone outcrops with access to an adjacent fuel supply (usually wood, charcoal or coal). In ovens with typically arched openings, the quarried mineral was incinerated, or 'calcined', at temperatures approaching 1,000 degrees centigrade, producing lime in a transportable powdered form. But during Victorian times the resultant 'quicklime' was required in industrial quantities, and the response at Marsden was in effect a lime-producing factory.

Magnesium limestone has been quarried in the Marsden district for centuries. After coal-mining commenced at nearby Whitburn colliery in 1874, it was then a logical and potentially lucrative step to intensify the limestone process. A new quarry was opened and a massive stone battery, strengthened with metal and timber beams, was built into its long embankment. Initially there were 15 combustion or 'draw' arches, but demand soon outstripped their capacity and within 20 years two new kilns were added.

To maintain profitability, the kilns were in use almost continuously. Railway sidings from the nearby pithead allowed coal and limestone to be fed into the kiln tops, while the cooled quicklime was loaded into trucks at the bottom for the downhill journey to the Stone Quay in South Shields and markets far and wide.

While mostly carried out in the open air, operating the lime kilns was hot, heavy and dangerous work. The corrosiveness of undiluted lime was well known. Before it was spread across fields, for example, quicklime was exposed to the elements, weakening the powder to form 'slaked lime'. Similarly, water was added to quicklime in addition to sand, for the production of mortar. Like most industries at that time, however, safety precautions in large-scale lime production were rudimentary at best, and contemporary reports of death and injury, by inhalation of toxic fumes and exposure to raw quicklime, are therefore not surprising.

Nevertheless, Marsden quarry and lime kilns made a significant contribution to the local economy during financial hard times. Through the depression of the 1930s a workforce of around 100 was employed, dispatching hundreds of tons of stone and quicklime each week. And even as demand from declining metal industries began to fall, production was switched to crushed lime, for which a new plant was set up.

It is often stated that the Marsden lime kilns were finally extinguished in 1968, coinciding with the closure of Whitburn pit. Local residents claim it was much earlier, however, as lime burning was overhauled by chemical alternatives in the post-war period. Since then, lack of maintenance and the biting North Sea wind and rain have taken their toll, and Marsden's lime kilns are now officially 'at risk'. Few would mourn the demise of a primitive and hazardous industrial process described by a contemporary observer as 'like looking into the jaws of Hell itself'. But the battered lime kilns – a final echo of a lost village and the generations who laboured there – would be sorely missed.

Souter Point

With the opening of Souter Point Lighthouse in January 1871, the cutting edge of Victorian technology came to Tyneside. Taking three years to complete, the tower's revolving beacon projected more than 75 feet above Marsden's cliff top and was Britain's first lighthouse to be powered with a source of alternating electrical current. Using a groundbreaking design, minutely detailed in local press reports, chemist and engineer Frederick Hale Holmes

Marsden's 'lost' village makes a fleeting appearance in this photograph from about 1900. Adjacent to the lighthouse can be seen the community's Methodist Chapel and Sunday School, which was built in 1884. Nine terraced streets were grouped behind it, housing a population of about 700. Their cliff-top lives could often be bleak and their reaction to Souter's fog warning – sounded every 30 seconds when conditions dictated – can only be imagined. *South Tyneside Libraries (South Shields)*

Following the closure of the pit and the demolition of the village in the late 1960s, Souter Point's lighthouse now stands in splendid isolation. Although its lamp was made redundant in 1988, the tower's two radio transmitters and aerials helped to keep an electronic eye on coastal shipping for another decade. In fair weather its distinctive exterior bands are now a beacon on land and at sea.

harnessed a 6½-horsepower steam engine to energise his latest magneto-electro generator. Eight panels of vertical lenses, the work of another innovator, James Chance, and enthusiastically described as a 'remarkable piece of optical skill', were then driven around a central electric lamp that, by using Holmes's replaceable carbon rods, produced a brilliant arc of light. Lasting 5 seconds, the ensuing flash was compared to the light of the sun and was said to be visible for up to 50 miles.

Despite such exaggeration, however, illumination of Tyneside's treacherous rock-strewn coast was without doubt an urgent necessity. An infamous stretch off Marsden was particularly feared. Some of its legendary bays and hidden caves were reputed to be a smugglers' and ship-wreckers' lair, and stormy winters rarely passed without the loss of men and vessels on submerged reefs or concealed sand bars.

After 1850, following years of political wrangling, the Tyne Improvement Commission began to implement long-overdue work on the river channel and Shields's harbour facilities. Trinity House, however, an ancient Corporation established in the reign of Henry VIII, was responsible for safeguarding the British coastline and building a lighthouse on one of its deadliest sectors. As designer they appointed James Douglass, later of Eddystone fame, and a site was chosen, overlooking the dangerous shoals and swirling currents of Whitburn Steels, midway between the entrances to the rivers Tyne and Wear.

Douglass's achievement at Marsden was based upon a cohesive plan. Not only was Souter tailor-made to house complex and coordinated machinery, but it was surrounded by an ensemble of buildings to support the main operation. Neatly placed around a courtyard, they comprised accommodation for the original staff, as well as an engine house and provision for ancillary storage. Sparing neither expense nor attention to detail, Douglass created a self-reliant organisation that functioned rather like a small village on the cliff top. All machinery was duplicated and the keepers were treated to the comfort of a covered passageway between their cottage and the lantern tower. Concerns were voiced about initial cost but this was a small price to pay for lives saved and ships preserved in future decades.

But change was forced upon Souter during the blackout of the First World War. The station lamp was switched to oil until 1952 when, for the sake of greater luminosity, it reverted to electricity. In line with a national policy of automation, Trinity House decommissioned the lighthouse in 1988 and it was closed and subsequently became one of the National Trust's most dramatically located properties.

In more than a century of unfailing service, Souter and its attendant fog warning horns must have prevented countless maritime tragedies. The light from Souter Point may be now unseen, but it remains unchallenged as a brilliant Tyneside gem.

6. Hebburn:
St Andrew's and Hebburn Hall

When Andrew Leslie first stepped ashore at Hebburn Quay in 1853 he was determined to make a lasting impression. Now his legacy is seen all around in the town he helped to build and the gem of a church he left behind.

The embryonic town was then little more than green fields and three coal shafts, yet the energetic Scotsman saw it as the ideal place to risk his £198 capital and further his boatbuilding ambitions. However, the 9-acre river frontage that he leased appeared at first unpromising. River improvements were slow to be implemented and the channel facing his new shipyard was waiting to be dredged. But Leslie was undeterred and his investment in Hebburn was soon repaid. Within a year, four ships were launched and his 'unlikely

Some of 'Leslie's Houses' – built by Andrew Leslie for his workforce and long afterwards associated with his name – climb the riverbank toward St Andrew's Church and Institute in this wintry 1940 portrait from the collection of Hebburn shipyard photographer Stan Forster. Leslie's progress in Hebburn was remarkable. In the decade following the launch of the three-masted barquentine *Clarendon* in 1854, his new business went on to complete 53 ships. For almost a century after it amalgamated with R. & W. Hawthorn in 1886, the Hebburn yard continued to build and overhaul vessels of every type. Shipbuilding ended in 1982, but Hebburn's tradition of maritime engineering has been kept afloat by A. & P. Tyne, whose ship repair and conversion company is now based on Waggonway Road, not far from Leslie's original berths. *Courtesy of Norman Dunn*

At 200 feet, the spire of St Andrews is reputed to be the tallest on South Tyneside. During the post-war enthusiasm for wholesale demolition, the grids of terraced streets surrounding the church were all earmarked for clearance. Some old houses have survived, however, and now rub shoulders with the new in the latest Hebburn Quay. Old and new photographs are taken from what remains of Hawthorn Leslie's shipyard buildings.

spot' on the riverside went on to become a stronghold of shipbuilding.

For a time Hebburn became 'Little Aberdeen' – named after the Scottish port where Leslie learned his trade and recruited many of his original workers. About 300 of them were accommodated in riverside houses, mostly of one or two rooms, some of which were lit by company gas from the adjoining shipyard.

Andrew Leslie was highly respected by his workforce. Around 800 of them attended his retirement presentation at Gosforth in 1886, and on his death in 1894 many escorted his hearse to Newcastle Central station before the coffin was taken to Edinburgh for burial. A memorial plaque was later unveiled inside the now redundant church on Ellison Street. In 1872 Leslie was described as the 'best saint' for his workforce. It may be more than coincidence then that a sculpted head of St Andrew above the church door bears a passing resemblance to the Scottish shipbuilder and benefactor.

Photographed in September 2010, Hawthorn Leslie's derelict office buildings on Ellison Street make a last stand against demolition.

Hebburn: St Andrew's and Hebburn Hall

In this early-20th-century portrait, Hebburn's own stately home has two floors of its reported 85 rooms on show. The steeple of St John's is just visible behind the house in the 20 acres of parkland donated to the town by the Carr Ellison family and officially opened in 1899. Ellison Hall was altered by John Dobson in 1819 and was famously visited by Humphrey Davy during the testing of his safety lamp a few years before. The Hall possessed a small brewery and a large garden, and a section of its wall now borders the town's bowling greens. In the foreground, posing awkwardly at the edge of the park Dene, are two figures. They may demonstrate that photographic trickery was practiced long before the digital age. *Norman Dunn*

Apart from the increasing screen of foliage, little appears to have changed in more than a century. The Boer War memorial of 1903 on the right was paid for by local subscription to honour six Hebburn men who died in the Transvaal. A globe of the world tops the grey granite monument and a side panel has a carving of an Army-issue carbine.

This advance party of craftsmen formed the nucleus of Leslie's workforce, which expanded as his reputation grew and his order book thickened.

Following Leslie's success, other entrepreneurs, particularly Tennants the Glaswegian chemical company, added to Hebburn's growing repertoire of industry. The swelling immigrant population – Presbyterian Scots, Ulster Orangemen and Irish Catholics – stirred a volatile social brew that caused unrest and sometimes flared into violence. But at the same time Hebburn was beginning to acquire the trappings of maturity, with clubs and associations together with educational and recreational amenities, helping to bridge the social divide and foster a sense of community in the fledgling town. As a major employer and increasingly a figure of authority, Andrew Leslie was keen to encourage such institutions – but not

It is difficult to see exactly where St John's church ends and Ellison Hall begins in this photograph from 1933. Hebburn's parish of St John was established in 1885 and services were held in local schools until the church was built. It was converted from a long wing of the hall and, when it was consecrated in 1887, the Bishop of Durham commented on its 'marvellous architectural transformation'. *Courtesy of Norman Dunn.*

before his men had looked to their own welfare.

Several years after their shipyard opened, and true to the Victorian ethic of self-reliance, Leslie's employees established their original Mechanics Institute. A single upstairs room in a worker's house was used as a makeshift classroom and library for children and adults. It was named St Andrew's after the Scottish patron saint, or perhaps in deference to Leslie. He waived all rent on the first building and in the early 1870s was the principal benefactor of a magnificent church and a more spacious public Institute accompanying it.

The new Mechanics Institute was opened in January 1872, built in fashionably Gothic style overlooking Leslie's then extensive shipbuilding colony. On two levels, it had classrooms with removable partitions on the ground-floor, and a hall, committee, lecture or activity rooms and well-stocked library above. Within months it was being enjoyed by a broad cross-section of the community.

Yet if the Institute was a valuable asset for Hebburn, the church built beside it was a crowning architectural glory. Again Leslie provided a lion's share of the funding, and the outstanding building, completed in 1873, ensured that his generosity would be widely seen and long remembered. The lofty steeple of St Andrew's Presbyterian church was well equipped with a peal of six bells, and equally well decorated with fine stained glass. Like many Victorian churches, its slender tower housed prominent clock faces, reminding the local workforce to be good timekeepers as well as good churchgoers.

Now the clock has stopped, the massed ranks of workers have departed and the declining church congregation has been absorbed by another Hebburn parish. But the Institute buildings have been restored to good use and, above all, Leslie's magnificent church continues to dominate the district. At the beginning of a new millennium, St Andrew's surveys a new riverside community and oversees the wider modern town. Hebburn is the living inheritance of Andrew Leslie's great industrial adventure.

Hebburn Hall

Rebuilt in 1790 around an already ancient core, Ellison Hall is certainly Hebburn's oldest building and arguably its most well-hidden gem. Tantalising glimpses of it can be seen from the town's main road junction – through a Georgian arch in an Edwardian side street, or shrouded by trees in the surrounding municipal park. On closer inspection it is no less intriguing, appearing to be a marriage of convenience between country house and Victorian church.

In the early 19th century the picture was much less confused. Then Hebburn Hall stood alone

Hebburn Hall, on the road to dereliction in the 1990s, and in 2010 restored and reoccupied.

and largely undisturbed among plantations and the parkland that archaeologists suspect has buried any trace of an original medieval village. Documentary records date 'Heabrym' to the early 12th century, and it was afterwards marked by a fortified building – possibly a sturdy Pele Tower, able to shelter families and livestock from the persistent Scottish threat.

On these firm foundations but in more settled Elizabethan times, a substantial dwelling house was built by Richard Hodgson, Newcastle Alderman and thrice Mayor. Fervently Catholic, he owed his fortune to the trading power of Tyneside's major town and retained control of his 'well wooded' riverside manor at Hebburn for several generations. But in the aftermath of the English Civil War he was succeeded there by Robert Ellison, another 'new man' and prominent member of Newcastle's merchant elite, but one who was to forge a much longer and successful association with Hebburn.

The purchase of the Hebburn estate, midway between Newcastle and the Tyne's harbour mouth, was an important staging post on the Ellison road to enhanced status and prosperity. By the mid-17th century, as prominent coal exporters and members of Newcastle's guild association of 'Merchant Adventurers', the Ellisons began to accumulate land along the Tyne's southern bank. Their income was boosted by fees charged to dump collier ballast on Hebburn shore, and increased by further land acquisitions until by 1790 much of the riverside strip between Gateshead and Jarrow was controlled by Henry Ellison, the latest patriarch of this famous mercantile Tyneside family. Furthermore, his new Hebburn mansion, on three floors, containing 85 rooms and set in landscaped gardens, was a concrete demonstration that the Ellisons had completed the journey from the commercial elite to the ranks of the landed gentry.

Yet within half a century the wealth that had brought the Ellisons to Hebburn compelled them to leave. At the same time as the Hall was completed, the first of Hebburn's three pits was set to work. Royalties from high-quality coal extracted on their lands were lucrative for the Ellisons, but consequent industrial growth made Hebburn an 'unpleasant' place for Cuthbert Ellison, who led the family exodus to fresher, less polluted fields in Sussex and later in rural Northumberland.

Nevertheless, Hebburn Hall and its outbuildings went on to play an important part in local life. At first, part of the Hall's spacious accommodation was leased to various businessmen. Towards the end of the 19th century, however, more ambitious plans were implemented when Ralph Carr-Ellison, inheritor of the Hebburn estate in 1870, generously donated one wing of the Ellison residence to become a church. The foundation stone was laid in 1886, and while the building of St John's radically transformed the classical symmetry of the original Hall, the church went on to become a cornerstone of the community.

Through the last century, other developments were allowed by the landowners to breathe some vitality into the redundant house and grounds, including a public park, cottage hospital and latterly a Masonic Club. Most recently, however, the Hall has overcome its greatest challenge when, after standing empty for some time, it was rescued for conversion to apartments. Farsighted in business affairs as Henry Ellison must undoubtedly have been, he could not have foreseen what was to become of his favourite estate and splendid house.

Opposite: **Wreathed in smoke, two Andrew Barclay 0-4-0-saddle tank locomotives approach the stop at Blackham's Hill. Taking the load is No 22 of 1949, while bringing up the rear is W S T (William Steuart Trimble) of 1954. Named after the Deputy Chairman of a Carlisle Plaster company, W S T has been at Springwell since 1981, while No 22 was delivered new to the Bowes Railway when it was part of the National Coal Board.**

7. Springwell village: Bowes Railway

On a long ridge south of the river, Springwell village is at the edge of Tyneside, but for almost 150 years its historic railway was at the hub of an immense coal-hauling operation. From the late 18th century, simple balanced inclines were employed where feasible to overcome Tyneside's challenging terrain of low hills and deep riverside denes. Controlled by what were in effect large rope pulleys, loaded coal wagons descended an incline, employing their weight and momentum to simultaneously draw up a set of 'empties' on the reverse slope. Operating the steepest inclines by stationary steam engine proved to be a major success and, as mining operations moved further inland and output from the north-west Durham coalfield increased, an enhanced and extended version of this transportation system was needed to deliver coal to the riverbank staiths.

Springwell, a stone and coal working community on the

outskirts of Gateshead, was the site of a new colliery and a railway designed by George Stephenson, which was opened in January 1826. At this time he was making his indelible mark as a railway engineer, having just completed the Stockton & Darlington Railway, the world's first public steam-worked line.

Close to Springwell was Mount Moor, a colliery network in operation since the early 18th century. A century later, this lucrative royalty was in the hands of the 'Grand Allies', a formidable consortium of

---

The haulage shed at Blackham's Hill, slightly to the east of Springwell, is one gem among many at the Bowes Railway Museum. On the summit of two remaining rope-worked inclines, Blackham's brick 'hauler house' is occasionally open to the public. Its original series of winding engines – all three steam-powered – were superseded by a 2.7kV electric motor. The 300hp machinery, built by Metropolitan Vickers of Manchester and Wild's of Birmingham, was commissioned in July 1950, and this photograph may show installation in progress. *Gateshead Library*

As the modern picture suggests, the surroundings of the 1915 engine house on Blackham's Hill west incline are becoming overgrown. But it remains a popular attraction on the Bowes Railway 'tour'. Rope haulage is demonstrated on special days after passengers alight at Blackham's Hill platform.

Springwell village: Bowes Railway

landowners and businessmen who sought to control the local coal market. Previously, coal from their Mount Moor pits had reached the sea by waggonway to the River Wear and keelboat to the port of Sunderland. But the Allies' new railway at Springwell opened the way to the Tyne's downstream staiths and London-bound colliers.

Yet the beginning of the journey was an uphill task in every way. Coal from Mount Moor had first to be pulled up a 750-yard slope by a stationary steam 'hauler' to the summit at Blackham's Hill, after which it was lowered down to Springwell colliery yard, almost three-quarters of a mile below. From there, gravity was again in charge as a self-acting incline of well over a mile, then one of the longest ever built, rolled the wagons into a marshalling area at Leam Lane. Because of a delay in the delivery of locomotives, the final stage of coal delivery to Jarrow staiths was completed with traditional horsepower until the summer of 1826, when a fully integrated system began to operate.

Tried and tested haulage practices combined well with the new steam technology. An extension to the line, incorporating further inclines, was made in 1842, and although individual members of Tyneside's grandest industrial alliance ran into financial problems, up to a million tons of coal per year rumbled down the slopes of their brainchild.

Even by the late 1960s, when shrinking demand and increasing cost led to the gradual closure of what had become known as the Bowes Railway, much of its basic principles remained unaltered. Skilled railway workers continued to make a difficult and risky task appear deceptively simple, as they ran to uncouple heavy coal trucks at the end of the line.

A segment of Stephenson's original line was rescued at Springwell in 1976. A Scheduled Ancient Monument, it now lives on as a working museum, manned by volunteers whose grit and determination to preserve this unique gem is as much to be admired as that of the men who first built and operated it.

8. Felling: Brandling Junction station

Standing unused beside modern railway lines in Felling's Mulberry Street, Tyneside's oldest surviving station is an historical railway gem. This tiny Gothic-style building was one of Britain's early passenger stations and the Brandling Junction route it served was in the vanguard of Tyneside's railway age.

Tyneside's public railways evolved from mineral-carrying waggonways financed by consortiums of entrepreneurs, colliery and quarry owners. At first horse-drawn, then supplemented increasingly by steam, the wooden and iron 'tramways' funnelled coal towards staiths on the Tyne. But following the success of the Stockton & Darlington Railway, proprietors also grasped the potential of fares in addition to freight, and the growth of public transport began.

In 1834, nine years after Stephenson's

Brandling station's little architectural gem is let down by an ungainly waiting room in this local press photograph from January 1970. The Brandling family were the district's principal landowners from 1605, and their Felling Hall residence was later abandoned, supposedly because of mining subsidence. But the site was stable enough to withstand the building of the railway station as well as the adjacent Mulberry Tree pub (now flats), which once welcomed its passengers. *Gateshead Library*

A modern generation of commuters glide past the former Brandling station in June 2010. They travel in comfort on Tyneside's suburban Metro line – a successful 21st-century tramway that is testimony to the staying power of rail transport. Operated on the system since it opened in 1980, 91-foot-long Metro cars are double-articulated and powered by 1500V overhead cables. Originally white and 'Newcastle cadmium yellow', their distinctive livery was replaced with a combination of solid colours in the 1990s. A further colour scheme is planned as part of the current refurbishment programme.

Stockton to Darlington triumph, the Stanhope & Tyne Railway, primarily intended to haul limestone and coal between Weardale and South Shields, became Tyneside's first public line. It soon branched out by implementing a passenger service in the following year from Shields to the turnpike near Birtley, where cross-country stagecoaches could be boarded. Scant attention was paid to passenger comfort, however, and after buying their tickets in a South Shields public house, travellers were obliged to walk some distance to catch their train.

Other developments were under way, including a route south of the Tyne, from Gateshead to the coast. Sponsored mainly by members of Gosforth's Brandling family, the Brandling Junction Railway was instigated to support their considerable coal-mining operations across Tyneside. It avoided at all costs the use of keels, which were condemned in an 1842 report as 'expensive and objectionable'. Conceived initially as a private venture, the scheme proposed to link Gateshead with Sunderland, via Felling, Pelaw, Boldon Colliery and South Shields. The enterprise received Parliamentary assent in July 1835 and a few months later became a public railway under the auspices of the newly formed Brandling Junction Railway Company.

Work began in August 1836 and the first part to be completed was between Redheugh and Oakwellgate by way of a stationary-engine-hauled incline and a half-mile viaduct above Gateshead's High Street. The company was also engaged with minor connecting lines, but on 5 September 1839 carriages were pulled by the locomotive *Wear* along the completed route. Felling station was opened three years later as part of a line stretching for 15 miles and costing approximately £327,000.

But the railway was dogged by misfortune. Over the next few years it was criticised for poor service and fell into debt. The Brandling company was financially overstretched and, as its shares plunged, was swallowed up by George Hudson, the notorious 'King' of the Victorian railway boom.

Nevertheless, before he fell from grace the sharp-practising Hudson (who was elected MP for Sunderland) was a prime mover in railway development. Despite the dubious methods he employed, there is no doubt that without his ambition and energy his newly amalgamated railway company would not have opened the first line from London to Gateshead in June 1844.

The Brandling station at Felling had played a small part in this railway saga. The station was closed in November 1896 to make way for a new building just to the west, but the Brandling line – like some waggonways around it – was integrated into a transport network that radiated across Tyneside. Most of its trackways have been torn up, but more than a century later a major part of Felling's first station remains and a rail service continues to run past it.

Originally comprising only a small office, the disused station building was restored in 1978 and for some time afterwards was used as an urban studies centre. Now a mere trackside curiosity, the miniature former station still clearly displays the Brandling Railway monogram.

9. Friar's Goose engine house

Isolated in a neat and tidy riverside park at Friar's Goose, the broken shell of a colliery engine house has survived from a landscape once bristling with industry. North-east of central Gateshead on Felling shore, Friar's Goose can be traced back to its medieval days as a salmon fishery. The origin of the place-name is debatable, perhaps alluding to local gorse vegetation or flocks of geese kept there by clergy from Gateshead's Hospital of St Edmund.

Without doubt, however, this small riverbank estate became one of Gateshead's first hot spots of industry. Shipbuilding was established by the early 19th century and Friar's Goose was the site of a chemical factory, and its 'most magnificent' chimney – 263 feet high – then claimed to be the highest in England. Yet organised coal production had begun in the area almost a century before. Two 'engines' are recorded at Friar's Goose in 1749, and the introduction of more advanced pumping machinery enabled a deeper shaft to be sunk in 1798. But after it opened, this new 'Engine

Thomas Hair's classic illustration shows Friar's Goose pumping engine at work. Reproduced from his *View of the Collieries of Northumberland and Durham* published in 1844, this is Hair's engraved version of his original watercolour painting. The Newcastle artist and engraver has caught the engine's might and shows the end of the beam 'protruding itself like a giant's arm' from the top storey of the pump house. In his commentary Hair relates how pit lads crawled out along the moving beam to oil its linkages. *Newcastle City Libraries*

Industrial activity has slipped into the background of present-day Friar's Goose. Aside from the pumping station hulk, only earthworks remain of Anthony Clapham's chemical works. A party was held there in 1833 to celebrate the completion of its huge chimney and, apart from many beneficial products, the site went on to make Phosgene gas during the First World War. No sign remains of the terraced cottages where police and militia fought miners in the 1832 'Battle of Friar's Goose'.

Friar's Goose pumping station at the turn of a new millennium – before the ivy took hold!

Pit' (also known as Tyne Main Colliery) faced testing times to come.

Inundation was a serious threat to Friar's Goose colliery and its mid-Tyne neighbours, not only from flooded old workings, but also because of the challenging geology of the Tyneside coalfield. Cascading 'feeders' from water-bearing limestone were often encountered at the shaft-sinking stage, and only their lining or 'tubbing' prevented destruction. Even after coal was won, however, seams often required constant drainage. Various methods had been adopted to clear shallower seams, including cutting of channels or 'adits' where possible, as well as using siphons and raising water by hand or horse power. But as Tyneside's pits were driven deeper, the steam engine came into its own as a water pump.

Thomas Newcomen's condensing engine made its County Durham debut in 1715, bringing with it a technology that speedily caught on. What it lacked in efficiency was compensated for by its reliability, and although greatly improved on by Boulton & Watt's subsequent machines (and indeed by the large 'Cornish' engines developed after the Boulton patent expired in 1800), the Newcomen remained the favourite of some northern coal-owners well into the 19th century.

The design of the last pumping engine to be installed at Friar's Goose in the 1820s is attributed to Gateshead colliery owner Thomas Easton. In 1844 the impressive machine – said to be 'the most powerful on the Tyne' – was claimed to have the capacity to extract almost 1½ million gallons of water per day. Until turned off in September 1851, the pumps at Friar's Goose prevented underground flooding across the district's mines. Estimated at 180 horsepower and with triple pumps, its great beam engine helped to keep five colliery companies at work in the surrounding Tyne Basin.

Disastrous flooding followed the end of the collective drainage scheme and, while other pits restarted later with independent pumping arrangements, the 'Engine' shaft at Friar's Goose fell into disuse. Resisting total demolition during the 20th century, the buttressed lower walls of the engine house have held firm. Ivy now grows round what could be mistaken for a picturesque folly. But this ruined gem at Friar's Goose once held Tyneside's mine waters at bay.

10. Gateshead: Central Hotel and Greenesfield Works

Framed by railway arches and flanked by sleek modern architecture, the Central Hotel is one of the oldest survivors from Gateshead's time as a railway town. The wedge-shaped building, often called the 'Coffin', was built in 1854 for a local wine merchant in an area that was also becoming central for railway engineering. Yet half a century before, Gateshead's ancient riverside district of Pipewellgate had staked a place in railway history.

At his Pipewellgate foundry in 1805, ironmaster John Whinfield diversified production of agricultural machinery to include locomotives. Acting as agent for Richard Trevithick, the erratic genius whose inventions fired locomotive development, Whinfield translated the Cornishman's blueprints to build an experimental engine. It ran on a short trackway within Whinfield's foundry yard, but never travelled outside and instead became a stationary works engine. While the machine was lighter than Trevithick's earlier attempts, it was probably still too cumbersome and broke the rails. But it had flanged wheels and was very likely seen by a young George Stephenson, then on the threshold of his own illustrious career.

But where Whinfield's

Barrels are being loaded into Gateshead's Central Bar in this illustration from its early years. Now a Grade II listed building, the historic pub is found on Half Moon Lane, originally known as Bailey Chare but renamed after an Inn that stood nearby. Designed by Newcastle architect Matthew Thompson and built for local politician and wine-trader John Cuthbert Potts, the Central public house became a hotel towards the end of the 19th century. *Gateshead Library*

Roof leaking and stonework crumbling, the Central is pictured here just prior to a long overdue renovation. During a revamp valued at more than a million pounds, the garish and damaging 1970s exterior paintwork was removed. In an area steeped in railway history, the Central's new owners – 'The Head of Steam' group – could not be better named.

Engineers from Greenesfield Works face the camera. Photographed in about 1900, these proud men and boys appear to exude confidence, certain that the railway trade would secure their long-term employment. Hopes were short-lived for many of them, yet until 1968 – almost a decade after the main works was officially closed – locomotive repairs were still being carried out in the No 1 erecting shop at Greenesfield. *Gateshead Library*

This comprehensive view of Gateshead's Pipewellgate area dates from the 1920s. Once a distinct medieval township, Pipewellgate was home to the aristocratic 'Gategang' family and named after wooden pipes that supplied water to it from the adjoining 'Pant Head Close'. It was slum-ridden by the 19th century and demolition began after the Housing Act of 1930. Clearances advanced up the riverside slope, exposing the fortress-like Greenesfield Works on its crest. *Gateshead Library*

venture eventually failed, other locomotive manufacturers were not afraid to try their luck. As steam engine technology advanced and railway 'mania' took hold, engine building became more widespread in Gateshead. For a time, an enterprise at Oakwellgate flew the flag for railway engineering in the town, but could not compete as development of land around 'Greene's field' – overlooking the river above Pipewellgate – began to take shape.

Greenesfield Railway Works, as it came to be known, was opened in the early 1850s by the North Eastern Railway, and by 1855 employed more than 200 craftsmen on the site, at first mostly engaged in engine repair but later in full-scale locomotive manufacture. Numerous general workshops, in addition to engine and boiler shops, were erected, which by 1896 provided employment for more than 1,500 men. Broad ranges of specialist engineering trades could be found at Greenesfield – including fitting, boiler-making and white smithing – and the welfare of employees was catered for by the provision of ample dining facilities and a literary institute.

Greenesfield reached its zenith in the pre-

Gateshead: Central Hotel and Greenesfield Works

war period when more than 3,000 men were at work, but alarm bells for the Gateshead economy were sounded in 1910, as the congested site reached maximum capacity and locomotive-building was transferred to Darlington. Some employees and their families followed the work south and the residual engineering operation struggled on until 1932, when closure further deepened Gateshead's employment gloom.

Work was resumed during the Second World War for essential loco repairs, but in 1959 Greenesfield was again largely shut down. Parts of its huge sheds were used for warehousing and car repairs, and some fragments have been incorporated into recent housing redevelopments. Gateshead East and West railway stations are long closed, but the Central carries on, a quirky and playful design in stark contrast to the plain-faced new hotel that now commands the area. Fortunately, many of the Central's original interior features have remained intact. Today's patrons can now literally look up and drink in the quality of the pub's finely panelled ceiling and decorative cornice work. They may also appreciate Greenesfield and the Central Hotel as handsome gems and a surprising reminder of a long-lost era when locomotives were made in Gateshead.

Demolition is seen to be complete by 2010 in a photograph taken from Stephenson's High Level Bridge. Pipewellgate is a now a wooded slope with a public art 'trail'. Amidst the pubs and clubs at the riverside, Brett Oils – established in 1877 – is Pipewellgate's last industrial stalwart.

Sections of the railway works still stand tall in Greenesfield. The former machine and tinners' shops now contain the stylish apartments of 'Ochre Yards'. But a small hotel, built at Greenesfield railway station and predating the Central pub by a decade, could not be salvaged in the housing conversion. Later to become part of the works, the hotel was part of George Hudson's failed strategy to establish the supremacy of Gateshead as a rail terminus. The hardly used Greenesfield Hotel was closed in 1850 following the opening of the High Level Bridge, and then Newcastle Central station.

11. Gateshead: statue of George Hawks

George Hawks was Gateshead's first and most controversial mayor. When he was born in 1801, the family business was firmly established and later progressed to form the backbone of Gateshead's economy. The thriving ironworks inherited by the young George manufactured a wide range of products, from chains to cannon balls, and poached work from its neighbour and great competitor Crowley's, which became outdated and began to fail in the late 18th and early 19th century.

It was therefore no surprise when George Hawks, described as an owner of 'one of the largest foundries in England', and at that time Gateshead's major employer, was elected to be mayor on 1 January 1836.

Reform of Gateshead's local administration was imperative in the 1830s. Faced with a heavy increase in population that an antiquated parish system could not cope with, the town's ratepayers reluctantly bowed to the inevitable and Gateshead was incorporated as a Municipal Borough in 1835. Hawks was predominant among the industrialists who packed Gateshead's original council and after selection as an alderman his later promotion to the highest office was unanimous.

But it soon became apparent that civic duties were not the first priority for the new mayor. With disarming candour he admitted that he was too busy to do justice to his new role, a situation borne out by his infrequent appearances in the council chamber. When he did participate it was usually to abstain on important issues, leading a distinguished local historian to condemn Hawks as a 'broken reed'.

His contemporary critics were equally outspoken. Within a few years of his election he was branded by his detractors as lazy and indecisive, a political showman who lacked substance or genuine interest in political affairs. Such insults failed to deflect his political career, however, and although he personally acknowledged that it was more out of deference than respect, George Hawks again rose to be Gateshead's leading citizen in 1848 and 1849.

Nevertheless, Hawks undoubtedly rode a wave of popularity in Gateshead, not least among his many employees. Like several other Victorian captains of industry, Hawks favoured a generally paternalistic approach to his workforce and built cottages for some of them. Although 8-9-year-old children laboured in his foundries, some later reported that they considered themselves fortunate

Gateshead's first Mayor, George Hawks, is seen at his dapper best in this portrait by the Bambridge Art Studio. He was satirised as a ladies' man and a dandy by detractors, who also claimed that after meeting his electorate the Mayor was sure to brush his clothes. Hawks could obviously dress well, but was perhaps harshly judged. Opening ceremony arrangements for the town's High Level Bridge, built by Hawks, Crawshay & Sons in 1849, were disrupted by the Mayor when he demanded that his own works band should play. In the event the Royal Train halted briefly on the bridge before driving on. For George Hawks on this occasion, his loyalty to Gateshead meant 'no band – no Queen'. *Gateshead Library*

Gateshead: statue of George Hawks

Hawks's statue on Gateshead's Windmill Hills is ignored by townspeople in this postcard view. For many years Hawks lived nearby at Redheugh Hall, but he died at Pigdon in rural Northumberland. Hawks's memorial was erected prior the building of a new civic hall in 1868. His statue was never to grace its grand precincts, however, and flanked by matching drinking fountains it remained in the relative seclusion of Windmill Hills.
Gateshead Library

Hawks still fails to make an impression on passers-by in today's Windmill Hills. Once common land above the Tyne, these slopes became Gateshead's first public park in 1861. A site of gun emplacements in the Civil War, as well as election hustings, a meeting place and fairground, the heights were also 'studded with corn mills', the last of which was demolished in 1927. After repair in 1999, Hawks's monument was returned to the renovated park and now stands watch over the former Windmill Hills Day Industrial School. First unveiled by Gateshead MP William Hutt, the statue is made from Sicilian marble and Pruddom stone and was sculpted by Joseph and Robert Craggs of the Percy Street Marble Works in Newcastle.

to be well paid and well fed, and anticipated an apprenticeship and future employment within the works.

News of Hawks's death in 1863 was certainly received with genuine sadness and his statue was erected, paid for by friends and employees, two years later. Pompous and preening though he may have been, there must have been something endearing about Gateshead's first mayor. Indeed, his fondness for public display seems perversely to have confirmed the independent status of Gateshead's new-found mayoral office and raised the profile of Gateshead itself. In 1849 Hawks inaugurated Gateshead's annual civic service, at a time when the town was struggling to shake off the stifling influence of its economic arch-enemy Newcastle, which it squared up to from across the Tyne.

George Hawks was a fascinating gem of a character. After 150 years and some repositioning, his weather-beaten memorial remains on Gateshead's Windmill Hills. Hawks's name has crumbled away from the pedestal, but he would be relieved to see that his beloved mayoral chain is still clearly visible.

12. St Cuthbert's church, Bensham

During a long and successful career, Tyneside architect John Dobson designed many acclaimed buildings, large and small. Among his 50 or so churches, St Cuthbert's, on the steep bank of Gateshead's Bensham Road, is little known and rarely praised, yet shares the simple grace that characterise his greatest works.

Initially used for common grazing land and quarrying, Gateshead's hilly Bensham district began to take shape in the early Victorian years. At that time, most of the town's population was jammed into unsanitary riverside housing, and Bensham was an airy rural outpost that could be aspired to but where few could afford to live.

Following Land Enclosure Acts of 1818, Bensham's fields began to be parcelled up and sold off, and prestigious merchants' villas were built there. Shortly afterwards, these were complemented by sturdily built terraced rows, homes to a growing class of residents – the shopkeepers and tradesmen who prospered as industrial Gateshead expanded below them at the foot of Bensham hill.

But spiritual nourishment was also needed in what has been called Bensham's 'select suburb'. A plot of its remaining land, formerly the Redheugh estate, which was

In a series of photographs spanning the centuries, various modes of transport approach St Cuthbert's church in Bensham. Here a horse and cart turns into Derwentwater Road, away from tramlines laid for the Gateshead & District Tramways Company, which began operating in 1880. *Gateshead Library*

St Cuthbert's church, Bensham

owned in the 1840s by the Askew family, was consequently purchased from them for church building. John Dobson was already known in Gateshead for the design of a mansion on the nearby Field House estate – one of his earliest works – and the 1837 renovation of the ancient St Edmund's chapel in the town centre. So, in 1846, and at his most prolific, the North Shields-born artist and architect began work on his next Gateshead commission.

The foundation stone of Bensham St Cuthbert's was duly laid in July 1846 and the building was completed over the next three years. Costing £2,000, raised entirely from public subscription, this relatively small yet neatly proportioned structure was built as a 'chapel of ease' to relieve pressure on the town's over-used parish church. This was often done in extended districts such as Gateshead, and when St Cuthbert's began a full programme of religious services in 1865 its Anglican congregation were spared the inconvenient journey down to St Mary's, Gateshead's original quayside place of worship.

However, as the population grew, Bensham's ranks of terraced accommodation were steadily extended and St Cuthbert's became only one among several other fine churches of various denominations. Like all of them it has witnessed turbulent changes in a town that has now largely shaken off infamous stereotypes as a 'dingy dormitory' or a 'back lane leading to Newcastle'. Grade

Traffic is now routed past a blocked-off Derwentwater Road and St Cuthbert's church, which is under repair. Although sharing design features with St James's in Benwell, Newcastle, St Cuthbert's marked a stylistic change for John Dobson. The architect was influenced by the medieval church of Barfreston in Kent, which he visited in 1844. *Gateshead Library*

II-listed St Cuthbert's became superfluous and held its last service in 1991. But after much controversy it has been restored and ambitious conversion plans for workshops and offices have finally been realised.

At first steam-powered, electric trams were introduced from 1901, and one is seen here descending Bensham Road towards Team Valley. The steep slope claimed four lives when a tram crashed in the winter of 1916. *Gateshead Library*

The last tram ran in 1951 and its ultra-modern successors are now regularly delayed at traffic lights outside Dobson's neo-Norman church. 'Go North East' operates the vehicle shown, as part of its Saltwell Park bus service. Its 39-seat 'Versa' models are built by British manufacturers Optare and are powered by Cummins ISBE, low-emission engines.

13. 'Underhill', Kells Lane, Low Fell

Between 1869 and 1883 'Underhill' was at the centre of a technological revolution that lit up Tyneside, then the world. During those years this large detached villa on Gateshead's Low Fell was home to Joseph Wilson Swan, the physicist and chemist whose greatest discovery was overshadowed by the controversy surrounding its invention.

Born at Sunderland in 1828, Swan began a career in pharmacy and moved to Gateshead in the mid-1840s to join family friend and future brother-in-law John Mawson in his manufacturing chemist's business. After the death of his first wife, Swan moved to 'Underhill', a house spacious enough to raise a second family and use as a proving ground for his groundbreaking experimental work.

One of his first achievements was to simplify the cumbersome early photographic process. In 1871 he developed a technique to

What appears to be rural tranquillity has caught the photographer's eye in an early-20th-century view of Kells Lane. Sometimes mistakenly believed to be named after William Kell, Gateshead's first town clerk in 1836, this area of Low Fell – a few miles from central Gateshead – was originally part of the much earlier Kell's Field Estate. Joseph Swan moved there in 1869 to continue his experiments and, as the photograph suggests, was unlikely to be disturbed by the encroaching industrial town. *Gateshead Library*

Despite Gateshead's rapid growth, Kells Lane has maintained an air of seclusion and retained many of its large detached houses.

'Underhill' was the first private English house to be lit by electricity. It was converted into an independent school called 'Beaconsfield' in 1928, and this photograph was taken about ten years later. *Gateshead Library*

Swan's former residence is now a care home for the elderly. On the right can be seen the metal-framed conservatory where the scientist carried out experiments. Most of the lawn has been dug up for car parking, and Nikolaus Pevsner's 1953 assessment of the sandstone villa as 'large and unlovely' has not yet been revised. *Gateshead Library*

dry glass plates, and afterwards he patented the use of bromide paper, paving the way for the popularisation of photography.

Meanwhile, alongside these chemical experiments Swan made the breakthrough that should have confirmed him as a household name. He had worked intermittently for more than 20 years on a practical electric light bulb, one of the holy grails of scientific enquiry in the second half of the 19th century. After experimenting with a carbon filament, Swan was able to add a more reliable power source and the fuller interior vacuum that proved to be key to the modern light bulb's success. After false starts during earlier demonstrations, a distinguished audience at Newcastle's Literary & Philosophical Society witnessed the full potential of this new phenomenon in a lecture given by Swan in February 1879. At the throw of a switch, a previously gas-lit room was illuminated by incandescent electric light and a bright new age began.

Other milestones followed in the wake of this. Mosley Street in Newcastle was the first in Britain to be electrically lit, and Swan's factory in Benwell, opened in 1881, is believed to be the first in the world to produce light bulbs commercially.

Despite this impressive series of firsts, however, Thomas Alva Edison is foremost in public perception as the creator of the ubiquitous light bulb. The dynamic American inventor worked simultaneously on light bulb prototypes, but was certainly influenced by an early scientific article by Swan, who went on to file a British patent for his design in 1878, a year before Edison. Historians continue to argue about the finer details of the ensuing copyright controversy, but compromise was reached between the cross-Atlantic rivals and the 'Edison & Swan United Electric Company' emerged in 1883.

Swan was later to relinquish his interest in the company and his reputation was eclipsed by the growing fame of the flamboyant Edison, whose further impressive discoveries led him to be dubbed the 'Wizard of Menlo Park', after the New Jersey laboratories where his hundred-strong team was based. Ultimately, Swan was eclipsed by an inventive genius whose greater resources allowed him to provide not only the domestic bulb but also the power system required to illuminate it.

Edison's British rival should not, however, be regarded as a lone and somewhat naive innovator, unable to exploit the commercial possibilities of his endeavours. Swan was in fact more of a shrewd and resourceful businessman than sometimes credited. His venture at Benwell thrived because of the astute partnerships he was able to forge with prominent Tyneside industrialists such as James Stevenson and Theodore Merz. The light bulb factory was closed after 1886, not because of failure, but to transfer production to Middlesex and capitalise on a larger market. Joseph Swan left Tyneside for the south to manage his various enterprises and died in Surrey in 1914. Tyneside commemorates his achievements in the name of Swan House in Newcastle and 'Underhill' in Gateshead where a 'blue plaque' is fixed to the colourful brickwork. Now hidden at the top of a tree-lined drive, 99 Kells Lane was a powerhouse of invention for Sir Joseph Swan, one of Tyneside's most ingenious and undervalued scientific talents.

14. Ravensworth Castle

Ravensworth Castle is now a mere shadow of its former self. The ruins of this once outstanding building lie hidden by woodland not far from the gleaming shopping malls of Gateshead's Metro Centre, built on industrial wasteland in the 1980s and presently reputed to be the largest retail park in Europe.

For much of its particular history Ravensworth was the ancestral home of the Liddell family. Newcastle merchant Thomas Liddell purchased the sizeable Ravensworth estate in 1607, and the original medieval castle, comprising a large courtyard flanked by curtain walls and four towers, was substantially altered during the following century. Two towers and some walling were retained by the Liddells in their 1724 gentrification, as they demolished the old castle and replaced it with a house that appears to have been large but undistinguished. Good taste was not ignored for long, however, and fashionable architect James Paine carried out various improvements, inside and out, over subsequent decades.

But with the ennoblement of another Liddell, Ravensworth was again transformed. The ancient barony was restored and Sir Thomas Liddell, friend of George IV, was installed as the second Lord Ravensworth in 1821. By 1846 work on his new house at Ravensworth was complete. His eldest son, Thomas Henry, appears to have been heavily involved in the design, although much earlier ground plans by royal architect John Nash exist. Yet whoever inspired it, a picturesque structure – masterpiece of English Gothic Revival – was eventually unveiled.

Retaining some medieval features but now sprouting romantic towers and embattled turrets, Ravensworth became

The contrast between past and present could hardly be greater than at Ravensworth. Reputed to be once the oldest fortified buildings in Durham, Ravensworth Castle can be seen at its pristine best and ruined worst in these images. At a time when John Dobson was starting out on his career, this 'monster castle' must have influenced his architectural development. The estate's lush parkland glimpsed in the photographs was at one time roamed by a herd of reindeer brought to Ravensworth by Henry Liddell, an 18th-century baronet and adventurer. Unfortunately his Lapland curiosities failed to survive one particularly cold Tyneside winter. While the castle's former grandeur is hard to imagine given its present dereliction, both castle and estate (now strictly private) were popular until well into the 20th century as a venue for day trips, picnics and regimental tattoos. *Gateshead Library/author (2)*

Ravensworth Castle

an archetypal fairy-tale castle. Its interiors were hardly less restrained, with a cavernous great hall and an imposing staircase that led to a 100-foot-long gallery and museum where Lord Ravensworth's valuable collections were displayed. Substantial wealth was needed to finance such a great project, and at its peak the estate was also equipped with private gas and water works, was serviced by numerous domestic staff and employed its own forester and coachman.

Curiously, Ravensworth's extravagant creation also became associated with Charles Dodgson, who, as 'Lewis Carroll', modelled his 'Wonderland' heroine on Alice, niece of Lord Ravensworth.

Unfortunately the Ravensworth story has no happy ending. The earldom ended with Athol Liddell, who died without an heir in 1904, and a furniture and fine art sale in 1920 heralded the demise of the castle itself. Eslington Park, a less ostentatious mansion in more remote and industry-free Northumberland, became the main country seat of the Liddell descendants, and their grand former home in Gateshead was briefly used as a high school for girls before it was abandoned to the elements.

A drastic solution for the already decaying building was greeted with public hostility in 1936. Citing mining subsistence, a new Lord Ravensworth proposed the building of a model village from the flattened debris of what he insisted was an irreparable structure. To the relief of many critics, his bizarre plan, branded as thinly disguised vandalism, was not carried out immediately. Not to be outdone, however, his successor demolished much of the fabric in 1953, leaving only the battered fragments seen today. A few new houses were built, but had the castle been spared and restoration investment forthcoming, Ravensworth might have been a jewel in the crown of Tyneside's heritage industry.

15. Dunston Staiths

Staiths were once common along the banks of the Tyne. These predominantly wooden structures were always susceptible to fire and this, combined with the demise of the coal trade and the prolonged neglect of so many industrial monuments, makes the preservation of any one of them all the more remarkable.

Dunston Staiths, to the south-west of Newcastle and within view of its magnificent cavalcade of bridges, are now officially recognised for their historic value and are promoted as an attractive selling point for the accompanying housing developments. Some residents may doubt the attraction of the staiths, a section of which remains burned-out and charred after a recent blaze, but most would agree that this intricate timber construction, 1,700 feet long and reputed to be Europe's largest, is an industrial treasure well worth preservation.

Coal staiths are recorded in local records from the 14th century, but Daniel Defoe brought them to wider attention 400 years later. In 1726, he wrote of a 'great storehouse called a Stethe', probably referring to the protection and storage of coal destined for the discerning London market. As that demand grew, more staiths were built. Their huge timber constructions, so impressive to Defoe, eventually became an integral part of Tyneside's increasingly complex mechanism for the transport of coal.

By the middle of the 18th century, with the opening out of the great northern coalfield, more than 50 miles of waggonways converged on the Tyne. At the terminus of their wooden tracks, coal trucks creaked onto pier-like staiths to discharge their loads, measured by the 2.65-ton volume of each

Sunset on the Tyne throws Dunston Staiths into sharp relief. Although the exact date of this moody river view is not recorded, it was most likely to be during Dunston's heyday. At least four colliers lie off the outer or river staiths, while another disappears into the gathering darkness of the inner berth. Coal trading with London depended on these tough little vessels, particularly the 'flat iron colliers' whose masts and funnels could be folded down to pass under bridges. *Gateshead Library*

Dunston Staiths

Trevor Ermel's dramatic interpretation is well suited to Dunston Staiths in their twilight years. Photographed in August 1978, a lone ship lies alongside the staiths while a rake of wagons stands on the top tier at the eastern end. Taking on coal is the MV *Storrington*, operated by the Stephenson Clarke Line, a Tyneside company stretching back to the early 18th century. Built in 1959, the *Storrington* was wrecked off the Yemen coast in 1984. As Dunston's work declined in the 1970s, the staiths' largely pitch pine structure was cut down to pile level on the landward side. *Gateshead Library*

waggon as 'Newcastle Chaldrons'. Delivery of coal to the waiting riverside vessels also became more sophisticated about this time. Defoe describes coal being 'shot' directly from waggon to keel, probably tipped down a chute or 'spout' that projected from the staiths' upper platform. This vigorous process damaged 'large' coals, particularly valuable to the London consumer, and in 1807 a gentler coal 'drop' was introduced at Wallsend. Attributed to Whitby-born and now overlooked engineer William Chapman, this used a counterbalanced platform to lower coal directly on to the decks of waiting ships. Coal-owners may have welcomed his clever invention, but both spouts and drops were resented by the keel boatmen, who watched their livelihoods being progressively carried away on larger coastal craft.

Despite this, manual labour continued to play a vital part in the operation of the riverside staiths. Well into the 20th century, although by then the process began to be aided by steam and electrical machinery, 'Teemers and Trimmers' were at work on the Tyne's staiths. These gangs of men laboured in hot and dusty holds, directing the flow of coal and shovelling it into place.

This was true for many years at Dunston, where in 1621 a staith is documented to have serviced Whickham's collieries. Dunston's

Despite a further attack by fire-raisers in July 2010, Dunston Staiths still exert a monumental presence. Once operated with 12 gravity spouts and three electric conveyors, the staiths are a last great reminder of the wooden workhorses once common along the Tyne.

present staiths were built for the North Eastern Railway in the late 19th century. Constructed parallel to the riverbank and provided with six berths, which were often full, more than 5 million tons of coal and coke were shipped from them at their peak. Following closure in 1980, parts of the structure were dismantled, but enough remained to be overhauled and provide a spectacular backdrop to Gateshead's National Garden Festival ten years later. Due to this and the latest housing scheme, an unacknowledged workhorse of Tyneside's coal trade has finally been given pride of place.

16. Swalwell ironworks

At more than 100 feet high, Swalwell's tallest chimney would be a difficult object to hide, though it hardly seems to warrant a glance from shoppers in the car park that it overshadows. But this lofty gem is a pointer to an area of now largely vanished industry, and the exceptional part played in it by Ambrose Crowley, Tyneside's first 'man of iron'.

Stourbridge ironmaster Crowley chose the Tyneside area to spark off his own manufacturing revolution in 1691 after the end of his previous industrial development further south at the port of Sunderland. His attempt to establish nail-making there was short-lived, said to have been caused by local animosity towards his mostly foreign (and Catholic) workforce.

People pause in the sunshine on Keelman's Bridge at Swalwell in this colour postcard view. Flowing beneath the bridge is a watercourse once supplying a series of local industries. First and foremost was Crowley's ironworks, the site of which is marked by the background chimney. The stream was filled in and Keelman's Bridge was demolished to make way for major road building in the 1970s. But for many years after the last keelboat had sailed away from Crowley's factory wharves, the small bridge was used to reach allotments in an area of Swalwell known as the 'Sands'. *Gateshead Library*

Just beyond the trees, the Sands is enshrined in the name of a modern industrial estate. The old river channel is buried beneath it, but the mill chimney stands unmoved. It was built to serve the Northumberland Paper Mills Company, owned by William Grace, who moved to Swalwell from Newcastle in the late 19th century. *Gateshead Library*

Possibly at the invitation of landowner Sir William Bowes, but definitely attracted by a combination of rich coal seams around Gateshead and water power from the 'rushing' River Derwent, a tributary of the Tyne, Crowley moved to the hamlet of Winlaton and by 1707 had made nearby Swalwell his manufacturing centre. From there the Tyne was easily accessible and keel boats plied the short passage to Crowley's wharves, discharging imported bar and pig iron and loading a wide array of finished metalware, including the increasing quantities of military hardware required to wage Britain's Continental wars.

After his untimely death in 1713, Crowley's works were regarded as one of the largest in Europe, overwhelming visitors with their scale and complexity. An inventory of 1728 indicated the high level of mechanisation on the 4-acre Swalwell site, which housed two furnaces and their associated forge hammers, metal slitting and blade mills. Yet for many years Sir Ambrose Crowley's contribution to Britain's industrial development was understated or ignored. At the root of his ability to produce almost everything in iron, from 'a needle to an anchor', lay

Grace's business did not survive for long in the 20th century, but his works chimney has been repointed to last well into the 21st.

Blacksmith Richard Hurst is framed at the door of his forge in Hood Square, Winlaton. A few miles downstream from Swalwell, Winlaton Mill was Ambrose Crowley's first destination after leaving Sunderland in 1691. Workshops were established in Winlaton village, which, though abandoned by Crowley's after the Napoleonic Wars, retained its iron-working tradition. Independent craftsmen such as Mr Hurst worked on until the 20th century, and the sandstone rubble building to his left – Willington Cottage Forge – can be visited today. *Gateshead Library*

Just behind the library, Winlaton Cottage Forge can be opened by arrangement.

remarkable technical innovation and expertise. In particular he was responsible for the introduction to Britain of shear steel, converting imported raw bar in cementation furnaces into a high-quality, more resilient product suitable for cutlery and other edged products. This process was not new, but so successful was Crowley's adoption and improvement of it that the material eagerly purchased in Sheffield and other burgeoning metalworking districts was henceforth called 'Newcastle Steel', and not 'German' as previously.

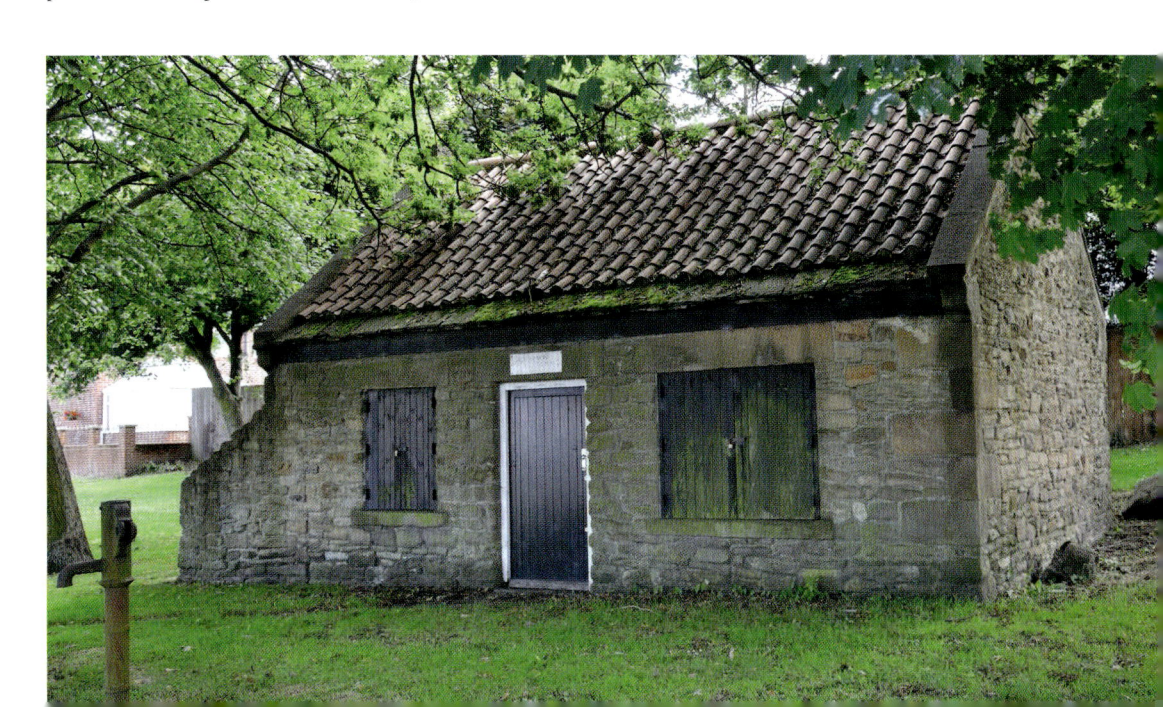

But just as significantly, alongside technological advance at his Tyneside factories Crowley adopted a unique approach to the integrated organisation and management of the men and women who worked there. Fiercely ambitious in business, he was nevertheless influenced by his Quaker background, and was a paternalistic employer who allowed his employees an element of participation unparalleled at that time.

Discipline was enforced by a strict code of practice referred to as 'Crowley's Laws', but there also existed a works council for the resolution of disputes. Enlightened provisions were also made for the health and welfare of 'Crowley's Crew', as his workforce became known. Ambrose Crowley's actions anticipated the welfare state by two centuries, with allowances for sickness, unemployment and old age as well as levies to lend some support to the community's poor and disabled.

Despite such apparent commercial and social advantages, however, the Crowley Empire was eventually brought down by the market forces it had done much to stimulate. After the loss of their dynamic founder, Crowley's successors could never emulate his creativity. In the long run they were unable to counteract the growth of powerful local and national competitors who imitated the Crowley works techniques if not their system of employee care. A long period of decline ended with closure around 1853, and although the Swalwell plant then passed through other hands, the site's weighty tradition of metalworking ended in 1911.

Traces of Crowley's great enterprise linger on at Winlaton, but Swalwell's lanky chimney stands alone, sole survivor of a lost industrial world. It is in fact a relatively recent arrival, built for the paper mill that covered much of the site at the end of the 19th century. Luckily isolated on the eastern boundary of the new retail site, the fine Victorian chimney remains. Around here on Tyneside Ambrose Crowley helped industry to begin its journey from cottage to factory.

> Axwell Hall is said to have been built to outdo the grand house owned by coal-owner George Bowes at nearby Gibside. At the time of this mid-20th-century photograph, the Clavering mansion had fared much better than its rival, which was then sliding towards ruin. A view towards the south front of Axwell's 100-foot square edifice shows much of its impressive terrace intact, and although not visible here, a garden temple built in 1817 stood nearby. *Gateshead Library*

17. Axwell Park and Hall

After 250 years, Axwell Park's broad patch of mixed woodland just to the southwest of Gateshead's urban sprawl continues to be relatively unknown, but has survived as a remarkable example of Tyneside's great coal-owning estates. It lies a few miles from the Tyne in the winding Derwent valley, one of the region's first crucibles of industry. Once prominently seen from across the valley but now almost invisible behind the treetops stands Axwell Hall, an 18th-century Palladian house held to be the best in Durham and now restored to some of its former glory.

Yet had the original design been faithfully reproduced, Axwell might have matched the finest and most elegant mansions from even further afield. Distinguished architect James Paine was displeased by the final appearance of the Hall, completed in 1758, for which he blamed the meddling of his patron, Sir John Clavering. Nevertheless, while the resulting building may have lacked the proportion of Paine's intended grand design, enough remained of the elegance for which his work is famed. Built as a three-storey block crowning the northern Derwent valley slope, the Hall featured a classical front pediment and wide terrace. Paine is believed to have been responsible for little of the interior

However, as shown by the broken windows, towards the end of the 20th century Axwell Hall was facing a threat familiar to many disused former stately homes.

decoration, but there is no doubt that Axwell Hall's stately rooms were a backdrop to the Claverings' business deals, as they navigated the murky waters of Tyneside's coal trade.

The Clavering family rose to real power after the restoration of Charles II and the reward of a baronetcy in 1661. Like many of the Durham gentry, the family spun a web of commercial and family links increasingly dependent on profit from the coal seams beneath their lands.

There were three branches of the Clavering family active around Tyneside, at Greencroft, Chopwell and Axwell. All had coal-mining interests in what was designated as the Stella colliery, which was in fact a combination of pits in the Axwell, Swalwell and Whickham neighbourhood. At the beginning of the 18th century this relatively small enclave was already undergoing rapid change as commercial power began to shift away from the guilds and the Corporation of Newcastle. Once primarily an agricultural area, the Derwent valley began to resonate with the clamour of industry.

But mining operations produced conflict as well as coal in this dynamic new world, and competition over what could be lucrative 'wayleave' rights was particularly intense. Coal-owners became embroiled in these occasionally violent disputes as they vied with each other to transport coal to the Tyne by waggonway across each other's territory. None more so than the Claverings, whose dispute over their 'Bucksnook' line led to its destruction and the brief arrest of its ardent promoter, Lady Ann Clavering of Chopwell. This outspoken heiress championed the Clavering cause and provided formidable opposition to the coal trade's most hard-bitten businessmen.

From the beginning, alliances were forged to counteract such hostility, and fortunes were made and lost. The 'Regulation', for example, was a price-fixing cartel, the

Axwell Hall is pictured in July 2010 on the threshold of a new life as conversion into 20 apartments progresses. Although some fine exterior ornamentation has been lost and the terrace has been stripped of its balustrades, stonework has been renovated and the 'Red Hand of Ulster' – the heraldic device displayed by baronets – continues to stand out from the building's tall front pediment. Dobson's ornamental temple is lost, but work is advancing to recreate Axwell's walled garden. This would no doubt delight Sir Henry Clavering, 10th and final baronet. Known as 'Mad Harry' from his seagoing days, the eccentric knight regularly opened the grounds of his mansion for local sports and flower shows.

Axwell's 'Red Hand' is frozen in stone on a restored façade.

precursor of a more successful partnership of coal-owners led by Lord Ravensworth, which controlled more than half of Durham's mines at the height of its power. As the 18th century progressed, the Chopwell Claverings and the Liddells of Ravensworth were certainly allied by marriage at least, and the Axwell Claverings became rich enough to move from Old Axwell to their new Georgian home.

They stayed on through the next century, when John Dobson was employed to build a north-facing entrance to the Hall. But the death of Sir Henry Augustus in 1893 brought the Clavering lineage to an end. The estate was auctioned off in 1920 and from 1925 onwards was used for local authority special schools. They began to close after 1983 and now, after years of neglect and vandalism, house and estate have become the subject of a sympathetic restoration and housing conversion project. The property developers enthuse about the exclusiveness of Axwell's 'secret' estate. Perhaps the latest occupants of this hidden gem will wish to preserve it that way.

18. Whinfield coke works, Rowlands Gill

Relatively few beehive coke ovens remain from the many thousands once found in Durham. But the preserved ovens at Whinfield in Rowlands Gill merit inclusion here. Despite being south of the river and thus strictly beyond the Tyneside zone, they are well-hidden gems from an industry that was an unmistakable feature of the landscape of the North East.

For environmental and public health reasons, the eventual demise of coking plants like Whinfield – emitting harmful pollutants day and night – was welcomed. Yet the process they carried out provided valuable raw materials for other important industries, and gave an employment boost to hard-pressed local communities.

Coke was a significant by-product of coal, and soon became essential to the iron and steel industry. Iron from early blast furnaces was contaminated by the use of charcoal as fuel, but this was gradually replaced by coke following the experiments of Abraham Darby and his son in Coalbrookdale in the early 18th century. The carbonisation of coal into coke also came later to underpin the manufacture of specialised chemicals. Similarly, waste gases were captured for further use, producing valuable distillates such as tar and benzol.

Whinfield coke works fills the valley floor at Rowlands Gill in an archive image vaguely labelled 'pre-1958'. A section of beehive ovens can be seen in the left foreground, while behind them is the Copper Oxide Plant and the power station. Built about 1900, the station generated power for the coke works and the surrounding communities. During the First World War it also illuminated an on-site factory known as the 'Alloy', which produced ferrochrome, indispensable for the manufacture of armour-plating. Gateshead Library

South of the Tyne, coke production and the Durham coalfield went hand in hand. High-carbon Durham coal was ideal for conversion into a quality coke product prized across the world. As mining developed,

Whinfield coke works, Rowlands Gill

many collieries, particularly in west Durham, opened adjacent compounds where ovens could readily be supplied with their coal. And to handle this, the characteristic 'beehive'-shaped ovens, although requiring regular maintenance, stood the test of time on the Durham coalfield. Even when outdated, their replacement by more sophisticated foreign designs was slow. Many beehive ovens were disposed of in the late 1920s, but those at Whinfield, built in 1861, remained in use for almost a century.

Throughout this period, coke production at Whinfield was in principle barely changed. Although improvements and elements of automation were introduced, the input of heavy manual labour was always crucial. And to be effective it depended on the keen eye and steady hand of an experienced process worker. Unless the coke was mixed thoroughly and 'slaked' by expertly directed water jets, for example, a poor grade or even unacceptable end product would result. Generally this was rare, however, and at their busiest Whinfield's beehive ovens dispatched more than 1,000 tons of premium coke per week, supplying British foundries from Consett to Sheffield.

As the 20th century progressed, other industries joined the coking plant at Whinfield. Such was the demand that a dedicated power station, using surplus heat from the ovens, was built to supply the nearby colliery of Victoria Garesfield as well as metal and paint manufacturers that came to fill the Whinfield site.

Coke followed coal and the other heavy industries into decline, and few traces now remain at Whinfield. Its scattered industrial estate, while important to the local area, is a pale shadow of the former complex. Yet shrouded in woodland and close to some factory units are remnants of the coke ovens that began it all. Acknowledged now by an almost indecipherable National Coal Board plaque, they were not only Durham's but also Britain's last working beehive coke ovens. Listed in 1975 and placed in the care of the Tyne & Wear Industrial Monuments Trust, they have been described authoritatively to occupy 'a small place in history'. It was a small place in the great history of coal, Tyneside's largest natural resource.

Only one chimney now disrupts the sweeping view across Whinfield's picturesque valley. Most of the modern industrial estate is lower rise than the works it replaced, but the terraced streets of Highfield village, once accommodation for coke works employees, still reach down the valley side.

Hard and hot work is here pictured in progress at Whinfield in about 1950. Tubs of small coal were first shunted over the top of the beehive cones, then emptied into the long ranges of ovens below. As loading continued, the fuel was spread out and raked level as the arched oven fronts were progressively sealed with fireclay blocks. To ensure optimum coke quality, the firing of the coke that followed could be prolonged – sometimes up to four days elapsed before cooling or 'slaking' of the coke could proceed. Finally, the coke was extracted by being scooped out on 'reels' – extended shovels that pivoted on overhead arms and spilled the coke into a transportation area. *Durham County Record Office*

Almost invisible in woodland and crammed up against a litter-strewn fence, Whinfield's last beehive ovens now find themselves in an unfortunate position. Of 193 original ovens, only five full and two partial examples remain. During the 1980s they were restored by the Tyne & Wear Industrial Monuments Trust, and can be accessed from Woodside Walk on Whinfield Industrial Estate.

19. Blaydon: statue of Thomas Ramsey

The first half of the 19th century was one of the most turbulent periods in the history of North East coal-mining. In deeper and more dangerous Tyneside pits new technology was strained to the limit, and above ground masters and men were in conflict as the miners' trade union became established. Some of its founders are well known, but a memorial to one of its first and most forgotten campaigners stands in the oldest part of Blaydon's Victorian cemetery.

Little is known of Thomas Ramsey's origins apart from his birth in 1812 and his lifelong association with the coal mines of south Durham, especially Trimdon Grange. From a relatively humble working background, Ramsey may have played a supporting role in the fledgling union, but what he lacked in prestige was more than compensated for by his enthusiasm for the miners' cause. From the earliest days he was said to be a staunch ally of Thomas Hepburn, the famed colliers' leader, who after years of simmering unrest in the coalfields united the pitmen of Northumberland and Durham under one banner for the first time. 'Hepburn's Union' of 1831 was defeated and dissolved, but activists such as Ramsey kept its spirit alive with his rallying call to 'unite and better your conditions'.

This was a time when combined industrial action could lead to eviction, and the yearly 'Bond' – the contractual agreement between collier and coal-owner – became a symbol of miners' discontent. As well as framing their working conditions, the Bond enforced strict measures of output and a structure of fines that could limit pitmen's earnings. It also tied them to more dangerous pits. With the growth of economic competition during the early 19th century, coal-owners rushed to exploit previously unattainable reserves and employed improved sinking and pumping techniques to win coal at far greater depths. Yet as the injury and death toll mounted, providing 'safety' lamps but neglecting ventilation proved no solution to disaster underground.

Tommy Ramsey fixes the camera with a gaze of steely conviction in this studio portrait. As well as carrying his trademark white handkerchief, roll of handbills and 'crake', the irrepressible union organiser was also known to play the flute as he marched to meetings. His hardships led to him being termed a 'sacrificed' man, and even when at last employed by the Durham Miners Association he was expected to live and run his district on a wage of 28 shillings per week.
Courtesy of Bill Dixon

None of the problems were resolved by the bitter strike of 1844, but Ramsey emerged as one of its heroes and continued to be a tireless advocate of unity. By 1849, with the slogan of 'better ventilation for mines, and the Government inspection thereof', the union movement began to stir into action once more. Over the next 20 years pioneers like Ramsey tramped around the mining districts, encouraging miners to attend meetings of their reviving union, attracting their attention with a loud rattle known as a 'crake'. He cut a distinctive appearance with his bushy beard, top hat and long frock coat, and although not a born orator his short speeches were rousing and to the point.

Over the years 'Tommy' Ramsey paid a high price for his dedication. Employers banned him from their pits and he was the victim of physical attacks. But his loyalty and courage were rewarded in 1870 by his appointment as assistant agent to the newly formed Durham Miners Association. He lived to see the abolition of the despised Bond in April 1872, but tragically died the following year after slipping on ice at his brother's home in Blaydon.

Miners from throughout the district attended the funeral of their veteran union pioneer, and in respect and admiration afterwards erected a commemorative statue. Dedicated to 'a zealous worker, a faithfull (sic) friend, a christian patriot', the sculpture takes up a characteristic pose. Thomas Ramsey was indeed a 'rough diamond' who is surely one of Tyneside's most hidden gems.

Sculpted by George Burns, the impressive monument to the 'miner's caller' now stands in Blaydon's Shibdon Road cemetery. With its pedestal, column and canopy, the memorial is 25 feet high and 5 by 4 feet around its base. So determined were Ramsey's colleagues to keep his memory alive that he was subsequently portrayed on several miners' banners. Famed among them is that of Haswell Lodge, which hangs in Durham Cathedral and bears the biblical verse 'They being dead yet speaketh'.

20. Blaydon: Path Head watermill

Before the introduction of grain milling on an industrial scale, independent local mills were a familiar sight on Tyneside. Powered by wind or water, their grooved stones steadily ground the flour that sustained daily life in the communities around them. Relatively few mills remain, but Blaydon's hidden gem is doubly important. Not only has it survived, secreted away in an increasingly rural enclave between two main roads, but Path Head watermill has been resurrected from dereliction to revolve again.

Bricks from Blaydon were world-renowned. Many were manufactured at Cowen's sites on the Blaydon Burn, and this photograph shows the 'low yard' near the Tyne. Before their brick-built success, Cowen family members worked at the Crowley factory, but their wealth was eventually a passport to Stella Hall and its estate, which Sir Joseph Cowen bought in 1850. His Jacobean mansion was demolished in 1955 but a brick summerhouse, seen on the left horizon, remains on Summer Hill.
Gateshead Library

Cowen's factory closed in 1975. It made 6 million firebricks a year, but the only sign of the lower yard today is a ruined kiln at the northern end of the 'Blaydon Burn Trail'. Recently opened, this mile-long nature reserve is scattered with industrial fragments and deserves its description as an undiscovered 'treasure trove'.

Hidden Gems of Tyneside

Rural life and industry were never far apart on Blaydon Burn. Pictured around 1900, this thatched cottage was part of the agricultural community that included the old Path Head Mill. The farm supplied horses for local mining operations and one of the houses doubled as a General Dealers. *Gateshead Library*

In common with most Tyneside towns, coal and dependent industries put Blaydon on the map (although Blaydon's famed Races also played their part). Mining is first recorded in 1628, and in the 18th century Crowley's iron factories based a warehouse there. Amongst later ventures, the brickworks of industrialist and parliamentary reformer Joseph Cowen dominated each end of the Blaydon Burn valley.

Yet long before this, several corn mills were at work on the Blaydon Burn, a stream that flows into the Tyne at the west of the town centre. By the early 17th century as many as six are believed to have lined the burn, one of them – the Stella freehold mill – in the vicinity of the present Path Head site.

Path Head farm was part of the ancient Stella estate, owned by the Tempests,

Blaydon: Path Head watermill

a family of Newcastle merchants, and a farmhouse and barn followed by the adjacent mill were built at Path Head around 1730. Some distance from the actual course of the burn, the mill was powered instead by drainage water from Blaydon's expanding web of mine works and waggonways.

Path Head corn mill was in use for almost a century, by which time its companions in the Blaydon Burn area were grinding flint to feed the manufacture of pottery and glass. Blaydon's booming industrial town, its workers' terraces stacked high on a steep hillside above the Tyne, was being built from the proceeds of brick, iron and clay. The coke and tar works that eventually developed 'Blaydon Benzole' – the world's first coal-based petrol – were also developing on the side of the burn.

Despite this enveloping industrialisation, however, and the move towards concentrating larger steam-driven mills on the Tyne, the hamlet of Path Head continued to flourish. A new farmhouse was constructed in 1903 and any remaining machinery from the original water mill was removed. After a period in use for crop storage, with the break-up of the Stella estate and the farm's final demise the old mill fell into disuse.

Nevertheless, the Vale Mill Trust, established in 1992, stepped forward to salvage this historic relic. Through its vision and enthusiasm, the Trust not only rescued a building on the brink of collapse but also recreated a functional water mill. After the overgrown site was cleared and landscaped, the dilapidated structure was reroofed and a new water channel excavated. With a reclaimed wheel and internal machinery from Northumberland in place, the sluice gate can now be raised to turn the water wheel for the increasing number of visitors attracted to Path Head by the surprising tranquillity of this picturesque gem.

Water flows through Path Head Mill again. After a publicity campaign and before it could be developed into a private house, the Mill trustees were allowed to purchase the site for £100. After three centuries, this area of Blaydon has now turned full circle. Surrounded by secluded woodland walks and picnic areas, a carefully restored Path Head watermill celebrates one of the oldest of all rural industries.

21. Clara Vale

Clara Vale, 7½ miles to the west of Newcastle, is a healthy descendent of the many mining villages scattered across Tyneside. Concealed in a hillside fold above the Tyne, much of the original purpose-built housing, disguised under layers of modernisation, is still in use. Although the original colliery-owners did not permit licensed premises, and it has no shops or schools, the small yet flourishing community of Clara Vale retains something of the independent spirit that made Tyneside's pitmen a breed apart.

While coal had been extracted in this area of the Tyne Valley for centuries, it was not until 1890 that the Stella Coal Company started work on a new colliery at Clara Vale. Named after the daughter of a company director, this relatively isolated place was previously referred to as Crawcrook Farm and Crawcrook Mill – an old flour mill, which overlooked an ancient river ford. The vale was chosen by the Stella company, which as successor to the owners of the Grand Lease Royalties was amongst the region's most powerful coal-owners, to further its expansion

A resident of Clara Vale's West View takes a break from tending his garden in a postcard view by Lilly White Ltd. On land at the front of their cottages, miners indulged their passion for horticulture. As well as a welcome source of fruit and vegetables, these long garden strips were also used to keep livestock and grow the fabled leeks on which pitmen lavished so much attention. Encouraging even more self-sufficiency, further land around the village was given over to allotments. Gateshead Library

Clara Vale

as surrounding pits became worked out towards the end of the 19th century.

These were years of comparatively full employment in the Tyneside coalfields. Consequently, to attract a new workforce higher-quality houses were built in Clara Vale. Even before sinking of the mineshaft commenced, a new road was laid into the area and preparations for the village were put in hand. East and West View were Clara Vale's first cottage rows, and each house cost considerably more to build than most contemporary colliery dwellings. Both sandstone terraces were stepped down the slope towards the valley floor and were erected within easy reach of the mine entrance, to the east of the pit head and its dominant chimney. As the pit became established in the final years of the 19th century, further parallel rows were added to Clara Vale, and the characteristic grid pattern of a colliery village emerged from once empty fields. These almost seamless terraced rows encouraged neighbourliness not unlike the comradeship underground. At the coalface the 'marra' system, widely operated by pairs of miners, shared the workplace and the wage.

Houses owned by the Coal Company and tied to employment in its individual pits were an important factor in mining life. Across the North East some colliery employees were provided with this accommodation rent-free. They were usually colliery officials or more important grades of manual workers, but a rent allowance could also be paid to family men, and other households took in itinerant mine-workers as lodgers to offset rental costs. The free or subsidised household coal traditionally included among these inducements was enough to draw in enough hewers, and by December 1893, despite wet conditions in the deeper seams, more than 20,000 tons of coal had been transported from Clara Vale's newly operational pit to the rail line in the valley below.

Not surprisingly, the miners of Clara Vale relished their leisure hours. Within

In May 2010 gardening remains on the mind of Clara Vale's villagers. As well as still attending to their shrubberies and well-kept gardens, community members have planted a 'Millennium Orchard' near the railway line to the north. They might be interested to know that village cottages that have recently changed hands for princely sums were available for about £100 in 1931.

Well-trodden paths lead to Clara Vale colliery, which began work in 1893. Costing £450 to build, its 70-foot-high chimney was in place three years earlier. Requiring only one repair, it lasted until 1952, when the colliery machinery was electrified and this village landmark was methodically dismantled by steeplejacks George Thompson and his son. Initially, six Lancashire boilers were in use at the pit and a pair of 0-4-0 tank locos were retained for coal haulage duties. Although slow to arrive and not long in use, pithead baths were added to the colliery in 1959.
Gateshead Library

a few years of the pit opening, village life began to blossom with the help of a Colliery Institute, football and cricket teams, and newly constructed Anglican and Methodist churches.

Most of the earliest colliery property in the North East was cramped and poorly drained with only primitive sanitary arrangements. Government regulations were imposed by the Public Health Act of 1875, but even the relatively superior Clara Vale waited until 1910 before back lanes with individual yards were built, and another seven years before lavatories were added to the cottages. All of these replaced the lines of unhygienic earth middens that formerly ran between the terraced rows.

In the 20th century, however, social improvements at Clara Vale were not matched by the economic performance of the Coal Company that implemented them. Stella Coal's glory years before the First World War, when output reached a maximum, were never equalled. Afterwards, in the face of falling demand, wage cuts and worldwide recession, Clara Vale, in common with the rest of the industry, struggled to cope with decline. Only with another global war

Clara Vale

did its fortunes revive, but in March 1966 the last shift was worked. Over the next few years scores of other inland pits in Durham shared the same fate as Clara Vale; closed in favour of coastal 'superpits' with wider seams more suited to the latest coal-cutting and transportation machinery.

But the village of Clara Vale persevered, even overcoming its designation as a 'Category D' settlement, the 1951 planning blueprint that discouraged further development in some former colliery villages. They were condemned to stagnation or even demolition, but instead Clara Vale has become part of a well-kept and admired Conservation Area. Furthermore, communal pride has ensured that the village has not been frozen in time, and in 1997, acknowledging the utility and harmony of its original design, a modern colliery row was built opposite the first historic terraces of Clara Vale. These old 'double rows' are a collective gem – a shining example of mining communities that were once the lifeblood of industrial Tyneside.

A short walk to the east of the village, Clara Vale's former pit is now a nature reserve. After two public enquiries, the local Conservation Group emerged victorious and ensured that this 3-hectare site would remain a community resource.

22. Wylam Waggonway

Cyclists and pedestrians now follow the tracks of many former Tyneside waggonways. Wylam is one of the most important of these historic routes, covering ground as rich in coal as the transport development it once fuelled.

Although it sits directly on the Tyne's northern bank, Wylam's distance from navigable water was an economic obstacle to overcome for the small village during the 18th century. Eight miles upstream from Newcastle, but too far on the 'wrong' side of Newcastle's low level bridge, Wylam Colliery could not easily tap into the growing market for 'seasale' coal. Instead, Wylam's coal was usually hauled in heavy carts or 'wains' by teams of horses and oxen that destroyed the road surface of Tyneside's primitive highways. Shallow-draught keels could reach the nearest coal staiths at Lemington, however, and the 5-mile gap to Wylam was closed by one of the area's earliest waggonways. These wooden railroads, in England first recorded at Woollaton in the Midlands, were soon exported north. Subsequently Tyneside, crossed by more than 100 miles of them by the end of the 18th century, became the 'home' of the waggonway.

Wylam's precise opening date is uncertain, but it was operational before 1763. Built by coal-owner John Blackett, it was possibly designed by William Brown, a local engineer known for similar projects in the region. Believed to have a gauge of marginally over 5 feet, the waggonway's timber rails rested on stone sleepers packed round with compacted ballast. Horses plodded along what became appropriately termed a 'Newcastle Road', and the waggon drivers, often recruited from nearby farms, were subject to the terms and conditions of the miner's 'Bond'. But in 1804 they could earn 3 shillings for three shifts a day, and on Wylam's level waggonway could expect none of the runaway accidents to which steeper inclines were prone. Their work could be as just as arduous, however, manhandling loads

Railway tracks are still very much in evidence in this late-19th-century view of Stephenson's cottage. After the closure of Wylam colliery in 1876, this stretch of line was incorporated into the Scotswood, Newburn & Wylam Railway. Despite healthy passenger numbers, North Wylam station closed in 1968 and the track was removed a few years later. In this view, the rails stretch away towards the station buildings and the remnants of Wylam's industry.
Newcastle City Libraries

Half a mile east of Wylam, George Stephenson's stone cottage is now well established on the tourist trail. Thought to have been built about 1750, the simple Northumbrian dwelling was formerly known as 'High Street House' and was once home to four families. Could the master engineer see it now, the tea room sign seen here outside his birthplace may not appeal to him as much as the 'horseless carriage' parked in his garden.

A working replica of Hedley and Hackworth's Puffing Billy attempts to live up to its name at the Bowes Railway Museum in August 2010.

at the staiths after unhitching their horses.

Improvements came in the early 19th century when fast-wearing wood, typically oak or ash, was replaced with iron rails. And at the same time as Wylam's colliery waggonway anticipated the modern railway line, around it was maturing a new generation of engineers who transformed its use.

It was during the colliery ownership of Christopher Blackett in particular that these 'Wylam Engineers' came to the fore. After 1800, when he became the new squire at Wylam, Blackett evaluated the cost-cutting potential of locomotion, and though Trevithick's 'Gateshead Engine' was unacceptable to Blackett, he remained impressed by the power of steam. Not until the latter stages of the Napoleonic Wars, however, when demand for coal was high and the supply of horses and fodder was low, did Blackett eventually turn to his home-grown engineering talent, and between 1813 and 1815 steam engines took to the rails at Wylam.

A series of experiments begun by William Hedley, manager or 'viewer' at Wylam Colliery since 1805, concluded successfully with some of Britain's first practical locomotive designs. Hedley helped to prove that with sufficient steam power and without the aid of racks or chains, coal could be hauled commercially in all weathers by smooth-wheeled engines on smooth track. His legacy was the *Wylam Dilly*, *Lady Mary* and the legendary *Puffing Billy*, which, with frequent modifications, remained in service for almost 50 years.

But other local men, notably Timothy Hackworth and Jonathon Forster, also significantly contributed to railway development. They assisted Hedley with engine construction and like him were gifted engineers whose talents blossomed at Wylam as they pushed back the boundaries of existing locomotive technology. And of course, Wylam's most famed son, George Stephenson, eclipsed them all.

Born a few steps from it in 1781, Wylam waggonway was in his blood. He followed his father into the enginewrights' world and worked at Killingworth during Hedley's most prolific years, a time, it is often argued, that spurred him towards his greatest achievements.

A popular tourist attraction, Stephenson's birthplace is now in the stewardship of the National Trust. But there is no fanfare for the well-trodden path that runs past its door. As much as any other on Tyneside, Blackett's Wylam waggonway is an unrecognised gem. Now part of a scenic Tyne valley bridleway, it was once a direct line to a railway revolution.

23. Newburn Almshouses

By the mid-19th century Newburn marked the start of a ribbon of heavy industry that stretched almost unbroken along the river for 3 miles east to Newcastle. Newburn village had ancient origins as an important river ford and, in the fashion of so much else on Tyneside, its future was shaped by the discovery of coal. Landlords since feudal times, the Percy family and their descendents, the Dukes of Northumberland, controlled the area's mineral rights. The Duke's bailiff, Hugh Taylor, financed the building of the almshouses that still stand in Newburn, not far from the historic

Pictured here around a century ago, Newburn Almshouses were governed by specific regulations. Seventeen clauses were contained in the original rule book. Most important among them was that chosen occupants – male and female – were to be 'of good character' if over 60, and if under that age be unemployed through illness or disability only. A weekly allowance was paid by the Trustees, but inmates would be evicted for 'immorality, drunkenness, or quarrelsome behaviour'. *Newcastle City Library*

To update the archive photograph exactly would now be a risk to life and limb. Yet despite today's busy through road, the historic almshouses are impressive from almost any vantage point. Originally fronted by trees and a 'neat' boundary wall, they were designed by the prolific R. J. Johnson, described at his death in 1892 as one of England's best provincial architects.

Newburn spreads along the northern bank in a quintessential image of the Tyne 'above' the bridge. Even here, at the river's tidal reach, the Tyne lives up to its 'coaly' reputation with dredging being carried out to keep a sluggish channel clear. The church of St Michael and All Angels, used by the Scots for their cannon in 1640 (and George Stephenson for both his marriages), overlooks the town. Towards the east, the lattice steelwork of Newburn Road Bridge straddles the river, while beyond it belch the chimneys of Spencer's metal works.
Newcastle City Library

parish church of St Michael and All Angels. These almshouses are an unexpected gem, gracing a place remembered more for industrial than charitable works.

Newburn's riverside coal seams were among the first to be mined on Tyneside, and after the medieval period the district became particularly renowned for the production of iron. Smelting began near Newburn in 1797 at the Tyne Iron Works, when sparks from two of Tyneside's first blast furnaces began to fly. But it was ironmaster John Spencer and his descendents who brought metalworking to Newburn and turned the village into a 'New Sheffield' on the Tyne.

Within a century of its opening in 1822, Spencer's integrated steelworks employed almost 2,000 people across a 60-acre site as Newburn travelled from rural village to company town. A row of 130-foot-high chimneys stood over the extensive works at the east end of Newburn and, among many other products, Spencer's record-breaking rolling mills turned out countless steel plates for the shipyards downstream.

Yet as well as dominating Newburn's working life, the Spencer family influenced its townscape in more subtle ways. In common with other major Victorian industrialists, the Spencers made some provision for the welfare of employees, and their factory hospital on High Street treated workers and locals alike. But the almshouses that remain on the opposite side of Newburn's main street are an example of a much older altruistic tradition.

Prior to the introduction of Elizabethan Poor Laws, almshouses were a privately funded response to poverty in England. Often established through the wills of aristocrats or wealthy merchants, these institutions are recorded as early as the 11th century, beginning a charitable movement that has continued for over a thousand years. Most almshouses were small establishments

In July 2010 heavy industry is a hazy memory on the riverbank at Newburn. The Tyne flows clearer and faster now, and to the west of the riverside park is a stone marking the medieval tidal limit. Although the large tollhouse at its northern entrance was demolished, the bridge built in 1897 stays in place. It leads to the Boat House pub on Water Row where, after more than a century, the bar remains open.

About a mile from Newburn, often unnoticed beside the riverside path, stands the old Tide stone. Badly eroded, its triple castle motif – from Newcastle's coat of arms – is now barely recognisable. But the late-18th-century marker is also misleading. A century after it was set in place, extensive work was done to deepen and straighten the course of the river east of Newburn and extend tidal flow well beyond it.

catering for the needs of a few selected inmates, and from the early 16th century onwards were typically constructed in single blocks with gardens to the rear and within easy reach of the parish church.

After three centuries, the blueprint was still being followed at Newburn. A long façade of 12 single-storey almshouses, with low roofs and high chimneys, lines the gentle curve of Newburn's High Street. A brass founder's plate, worn thin by decades of polishing, informs the visitor that the houses were erected in 1870, by endowment of Hugh Taylor of Earsdon. This 'influential gentleman', who had died two years earlier, was land agent to the Duke of Northumberland and a coal-owner in his own right. The almshouses commemorate neither of them, however, but are dedicated to the memory of Taylor's parents, who had lived in Newburn for many years.

Still managed by an almshouse charity, the buildings continue to add an elegant touch to Newburn. They show that the hard face of Victorian capitalism could have a softer side.

24. Lemington glass cone

In the 17th century, smoke from Tyneside's glass cones began to drift across the area. Some of these characteristically British industrial structures – a combination of central furnace and surrounding workshop – were established along the northern bank of the river. The largest cone, at Lemington, just to the west of Newcastle, has outlasted them all.

Before the first of Tyneside's 'glasshouses' were built in the Ouseburn district of Newcastle, British glass-making was largely a southern concern. When depleted stocks of lowland timber became more important for warships than drinking vessels, however, North East 'sea cole' became the chosen fuel for glass manufacturing. Granted a glass-making monopoly, Welsh-born Sir Robert Mansell – Admiralty Treasurer and afterwards Vice Admiral of England – set up three Newcastle glasshouses about 1618, starting a local industry that persevered for more than three centuries.

As Tyneside's glass industry bloomed, only coal-mining was more prosperous. By the closing decades of the 18th century, demand for glass continued to rise and glass-making capacity along the Tyne riverbanks almost doubled to keep pace. Consequently, in 1787, on a site leased from the Duke of

Lemington's 'High' cone lives up to its name in this Newcastle City Engineer's photograph from 2 March 1976. Even higher in the background are the cooling towers of Stella South's now demolished power station. At 240 feet high, the four towers have been described as 'brick cathedrals'. *Newcastle City Library*

Northumberland, Lemington's new works opened for the production of flat glass.

Lemington-on-Tyne was clearly viewed by the owners of the newly formed Northumberland Glass Company to be a prime location for their business. Four miles west of Newcastle's old town walls, this small village was at the junction of the waggonway and keel routes required to supply the glass melting pots with alkali, sand, clay and coal.

In 1797 Lemington's largest cone, more than 100 feet high and 60 feet in diameter, took shape. Within its cavernous interior, glass-makers carried out their ancient art,

Lemington glass cone

jealously guarding trade secrets believed to have been handed down by refugee Huguenot artisans. Hand glass-blowing in particular has always required exceptional skills. A molten glass globule at over 1,000 degrees centigrade, drawn from the furnace at the end of the 'blowing iron', is blown and cut by the glass craftsman into various forms. Annealing hearths set round the inner wall of glass-making cones were used to reheat the glass in a manufacturing process that defied change. Indeed, the process to replace a glass melting pot, practised at Lemington's glassworks until well into the 20th century, has been described as 'gothic'.

Yet despite such anachronism, Lemington glassworks remained open, producing specialised glassware until closure in 1997. Through a long life it underwent several changes of ownership and cycles of prosperity and decline. Following the failure of the original company in 1837, Lemington's fate was in the hands of Joseph Lamb, then the Sowerby family, who made their name famous with the introduction of 'pressed glass' during the 1840s. But both glass-making concerns were affected by trade depressions and the march of automation.

Nevertheless, Lemington was given a bright new start in 1906 by the General Electrical Company, which enlarged and refitted the works to mass-produce light bulbs and tubes and, before trade again subsided after 1960, employed almost 700 people. After the glassworks was demolished at the end of the last century, the Lemington cone was left in splendid isolation – an ungainly building that has since been used as an unorthodox showroom for cars and ovens. Among only four left standing in Britain, Lemington's 'High' glass cone is now a nationally important industrial monument and a gem difficult to ignore. More importantly, it is a symbol of an undervalued industry that was at the roots of Tyneside's industrial growth.

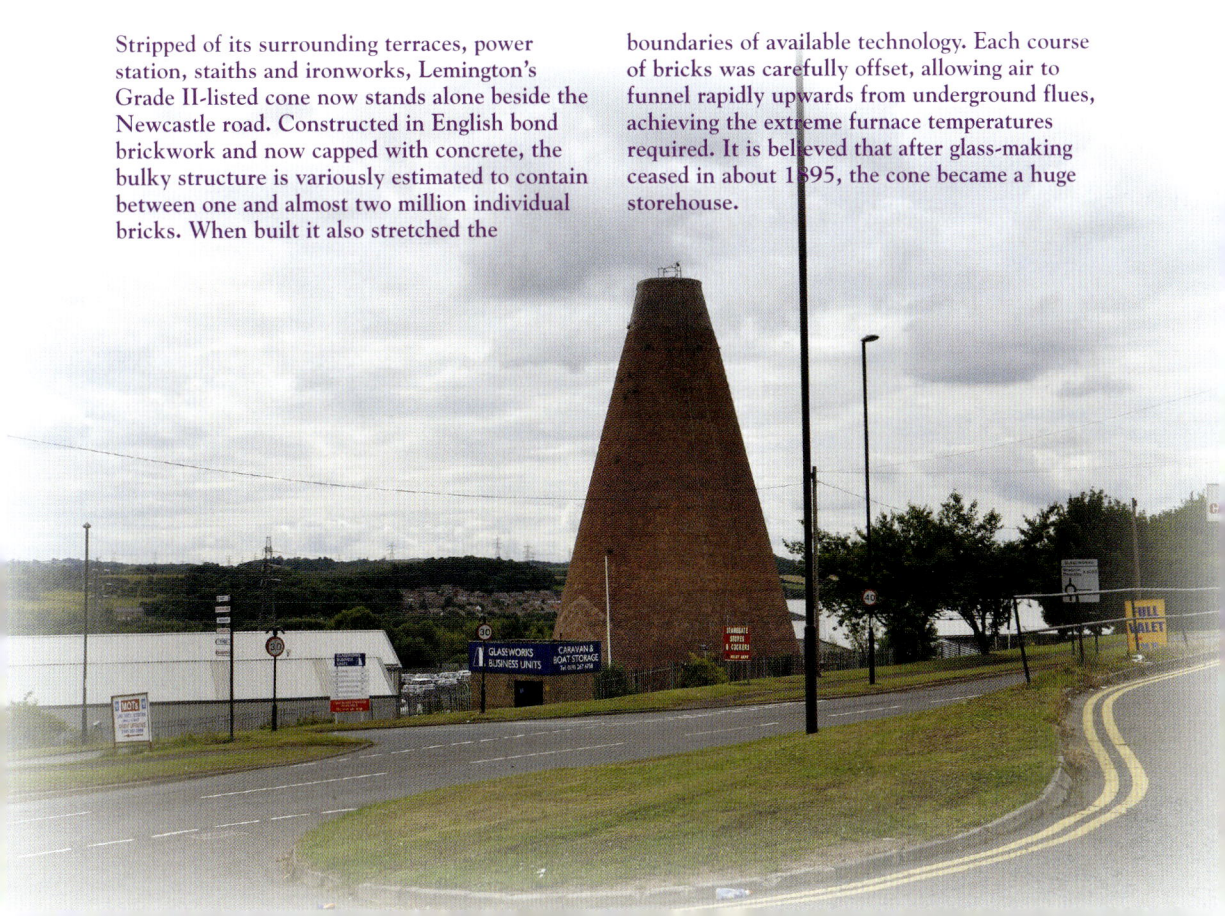

Stripped of its surrounding terraces, power station, staiths and ironworks, Lemington's Grade II-listed cone now stands alone beside the Newcastle road. Constructed in English bond brickwork and now capped with concrete, the bulky structure is variously estimated to contain between one and almost two million individual bricks. When built it also stretched the boundaries of available technology. Each course of bricks was carefully offset, allowing air to funnel rapidly upwards from underground flues, achieving the extreme furnace temperatures required. It is believed that after glass-making ceased in about 1895, the cone became a huge storehouse.

25. Elswick leadworks

Originally a small settlement to the west of Newcastle city centre, Elswick at the beginning of the 20th century was primarily renowned for Armstrong's huge ship and armaments complex that ranged for more than a mile along the banks of the Tyne. Lord Armstrong – arguably Tyneside's best-known industrialist – opened his works at Elswick in 1847, at first manufacturing hydraulic cranes before progressing to bridges, artillery pieces and warships. At his death in 1900 an engineering empire that had begun with 25 men employed more than 25,000 and Elswick's total population had swollen to almost twice that number.

Yet other industries had preceded the 'Great Gun Maker' to Elswick. Coal mines leased from the Prior of Tynemouth are documented from the Middle Ages, and stone quarrying was also under way at that time. Bleach, glue and other unpleasant substances

The days of Elswick's lead shot tower were numbered when this photo was taken in May 1968. Apart from needing repair, the disused tower, seen on the right, did not fit in with corporate expansion plans. Owners Cookson & Walker combined with other lead-makers to become Associated Lead Manufacturers, and after the tower was demolished the powerful new conglomerate made Newcastle its centre of operations. Included in the line-up of vehicles outside part of the original 18th-century office and accommodation complex at Elswick are a Morris Oxford, a Wolseley 690 and a Ford Zephyr 6.

were later produced, but even before Armstrong's enterprise came to dominate the district, Elswick's landscape was singled out by a leadworks and the brick column that towered over it.

Elswick's 174-foot-high lead shot tower could not fail to become a major local

Elswick leadworks

landmark. Appearing more like a lighthouse than an industrial structure, the spindly cylinder, topped by a vented cupola, was claimed by an early-19th-century historian of Newcastle to be visible from the Chester-le-Street area of County Durham, about 8 miles to the south.

Surprisingly for a region so rich in high-quality deposits of lead ore, local manufacture of lead products was comparatively slow to start. The important role played by the North East in the national lead trade is sometimes overlooked, but by the middle of the 19th century the world relied on British lead, the majority of it supplied from the North Pennine dales of Northumberland and Durham. Newcastle merchant William Blackett set up the Blackett-Beaumont Lead Company in 1684, but it was not until 1778 that a Hull consortium, Walkers, Fishwick & Company, established its leadworks at Elswick.

Its white, red and rolled lead, as well as paint, was in great demand, turning enough profit to build the lead shot tower in the closing years of the 18th century. A worker known as a 'shot runner' climbed the tower's finely constructed spiral staircase to melt lead in a furnace, then drip it steadily through a long handled griddle (a process patented in 1782 by Bristol tradesman William Watts). Gravity took charge after the lead was 'dropped', cooling and hardening into pellets as it plunged 150 feet into a timber vat containing about 600 gallons of water on a platform at the base of the shaft. After the water tub was drained, the shot was dried on a hot plate and graded by size, before polishing and packing for final distribution. At a time when Armstrong's nearby Elswick Works was arming the world with heavy-calibre weapons, the majority of lead shot produced in the tower became ammunition for rather smaller-bore guns.

Shot manufacture in the tower ended in 1951, but despite being protected afterwards as a listed monument, the tower could not defy the force of gravity. Even when constructed the shot tower began to tilt and, although this was corrected immediately, much later subsidence helped to bring it down. Had it not been demolished in January 1969, Elswick's lead shot tower would have been unique on Tyneside and rare in Britain.

In 2010 the leadworks site on Shot Factory Lane awaits redevelopment. Modernisation continued after it became part of the Calder group, and as late as 1999 the factory was producing an array of lead products at a rate of 15 tons per hour. An area of Elswick that echoed to the sound of heavy industry is now home to the 'Arena', opened in 1995 as Newcastle's largest sports and concert venue. Not far away a slick business park attempts to fill the shoes of Armstrong's giant engineering works, but few clues of the lead shot tower – Elswick's 'singular edifice' – remain.

26. Victoria Tunnel, Newcastle

The Victoria Tunnel must be Newcastle's best-hidden gem. Burrowing under busy streets, it was a neat solution to the problems of a developing coal enterprise as it encountered an expanding town.

During the 1830s Newcastle's urban layout was spectacularly gaining ground. Commercial euphoria following the Napoleonic War gave rise to a business and property boom that ended with what is now popularly termed 'Grainger Town', an adventurous redevelopment by local builder and entrepreneur Richard Grainger. His ambitious vision transformed medieval Newcastle and gave it a new town centre, distinguished by elegant street architecture still admired today.

Yet as an army of construction workers were completing Grainger's 'City of Palaces', more down-to-earth excavations were beginning nearby. Spare capital investment also gave a new lease of life to some of the ageing coal operations and redundant pits that surrounded Newcastle at that time. Among them was Spital Tongues, its name derived from an ancient tract of land once

The Victoria Tunnel disappears into the gloom in a photograph from March 1975, taken by Newcastle City Engineers on an inspection tour that found the 133-year-old shaft to be in generally sound condition. The metal tracks on view were laid in wartime, carrying away spoil from seven new entrances constructed at that time. On the whole, Tynesiders endured the tunnel's discomfort good-naturedly during air raids. For them it was definitely 'better damp than dead'. *Newcastle City Library*

Victoria Tunnel, Newcastle

the site of a leper hospital. It had been mined sporadically, but in 1835 a much more comprehensive operation began. After negotiating a 31-year lease, the company of Porter & Latimer opened a new colliery there to extract coal from beneath the broad wedge of moorland to the north of Grainger's fine upper town. However, Newcastle's Freemen – an historic body who even today act as Town Moor custodians – denied direct access to crucial quayside staiths, refusing permission for a waggonway to cross their cherished grazing pastures. Yet what could not pass over the moor and was blocked by the spreading town, could demonstrably go under it. 'Kitty's Drift' was an even longer subterranean tunnel opened in 1796 to link Kenton at the west end of Newcastle to Scotswood on the Tyne.

Work on the Spital Tongues tunnel commenced in June 1839, engineered by W. Gilhespie and supervised by Yorkshire lead-miner John Cherry. Later to be celebrated in verse and song as the 'best undertakin' that's been in the North', the tunnel progressed well, confounding some initial derision aimed at the project's 'foolish' owner. Although much of its success appears to be fortuitous – encountering clay rather than rock and following the course of old streambeds – Mr Porter's tunnel was constructed using the most up-to-date building techniques then available.

Beginning on the surface at the pithead, the completed arched tunnel was approximately 7½ feet high and just over 6 feet wide. Reaching a depth of 85 feet, it descended over a length of about a mile and

Excavations are seen here in progress on Claremont Road for one of the 18 new tunnel entrances actually planned in 1939. After delays caused by outdated surveys, the old tunnel was eventually reached and the occasion celebrated with drinks all round. Newcastle City Library

a half, through a 222-foot incline, until it emerged onto a pair of staiths on the Tyne waterfront. A single-track railway of 4ft 8in gauge transported custom-made wagons loaded with the standard Newcastle chaldron of 53cwt. With little room to spare, they rolled through the tunnel to be unloaded and afterwards hauled home by a 40-horsepower stationary engine at the colliery end.

Officially opened to noisy celebrations in the early part of 1842, the Victoria Tunnel unfortunately did not reign as long as the young monarch it was named to honour. Like the unfortunate Richard Grainger, its owners suffered a financial collapse. Despite the tunnel's high specification and impressive performance – greatly reducing coal transportation costs – the whole enterprise ran into difficulties after barely more than a decade. A banking crisis finished it off and, after failing to be sold in late 1859, the plant and equipment from Spital Tongue colliery and its tunnel were broken up for a public auction sale.

For almost 80 years the tunnel lay abandoned until pressed into war service in 1939. At a cost of £37,000, some damp-proofing was attempted and it was provided with extra entrances, electric lighting and a new floor, and, with the protection of blast walls, could shelter 9,000 people during an air raid. Since then, apart from reinforcement for the building of Newcastle's underground Metro line in 1978, the tunnel has attracted little attention. Although badly distorted in places by modern surface work, much of its tidy brick and stonework remains remarkably intact. Belatedly listed in 2004, this undercover gem is also a testament to local builder David Nixon, whose firm in Prudhoe Street, Newcastle, lay almost on top of his sturdy construction.

Glimpses of his handiwork can again be seen in a short section of Newcastle's Victoria Tunnel – a true buried treasure – which is now occasionally opened for guided tours.

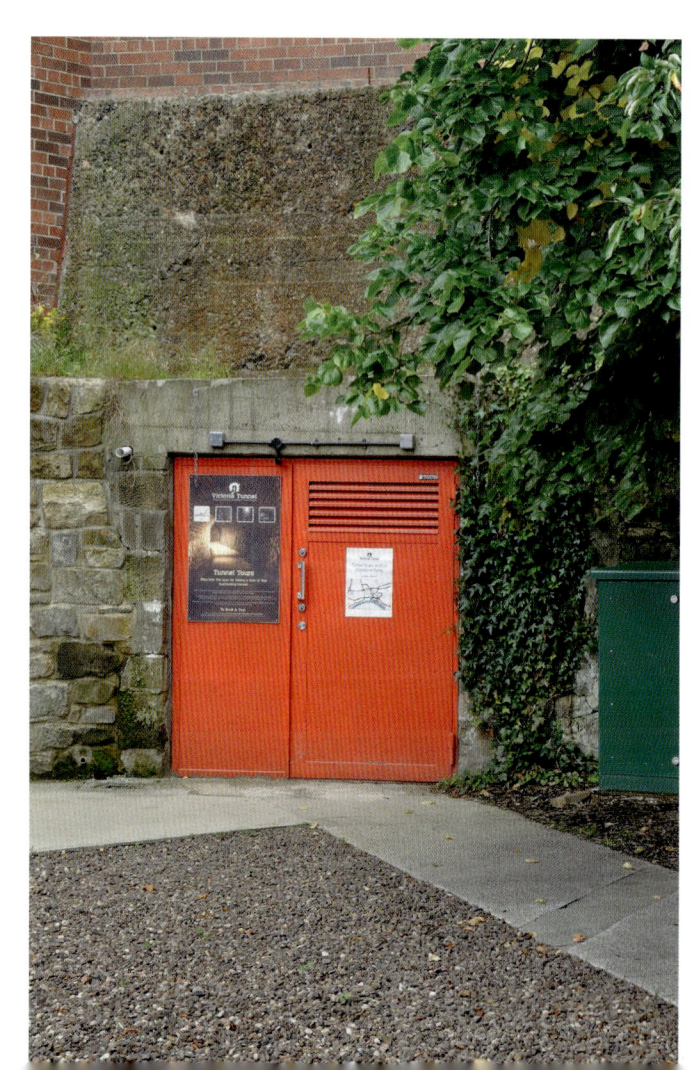

A ventilated doorway now leads to 'Newcastle's Hidden Heritage'. This entrance on the Lower Ouseburn's Ouse Street is the tunnel's last remaining public access point. On special opening days, torches are provided to explore a 766-yard section of the Victoria Tunnel, which was awarded £200,000 for refurbishment from the Heritage Lottery Fund in 2006. As well as its better-known uses, the dark and dank former underground waggonway was the location for a mushroom farm, which inexplicably failed during the late 1920s.

27. Windmill at Chimney Mill

Windmills may be far from the mind of students today, but Newcastle's 'Chimney Mill', near the University on Claremont Road, is a valuable gem well worth studying.

Long before the age of steam and electricity, wind was a power in the land. The first documented English windmill was at Bury St Edmunds in 1191, and the first in Northumberland dates from about 1200. Many once stood around the 'hilly town' of Newcastle, and antiquarian R. J. Charleton writes lyrically about their picturesque charms as well as illustrating the dangers of controlling these unwieldy machines. Apart from the obvious perils associated with setting their heavy internal mechanism, failure to properly rig and adjust the exterior sails in a brisk prevailing wind could result in damage to a mill and in some cases death to the miller.

Globe-topped petrol pumps await customers at Mundill & Watson's garage in Spital Tongues. But these were early days for motorcars, and garage-owners hedged their bets. A convenient mound of hay at the garage door suggests that horse-drawn coach and cart repairs were still carried out. Just in front are tramlines from Newcastle's 40-mile network, completed in 1900. But Smeaton's windmill – pictured here after its unique sail configuration was removed in 1924 – remains the main attraction and completes Claremont Road's four ages of motive power. *Newcastle City Library.*

Both the windmill and the church of St Luke's have stood the test of time relatively well. Dedicated in 1886, St Luke's continues in an active community role. 'Windmill Court' now covers the garage site, which until the 1970s maintained the motor trade tradition. When Mundill's moved to Jesmond Road, Northern Coachbuilders made bus bodies at the Chimney Mill site.

Technical difficulties such as these were a source of inspiration to John Smeaton, however, who erected Tyneside's first five-'wand' 'smock' windmill in 1782. Described by Samuel Smiles as a 'born mechanic', Yorkshireman Smeaton was supremely well qualified for the task. Often regarded as the founder of the civil engineering profession, he designed prolifically – from scientific instruments to dams and canals, from steam engines to bridges and the Eddystone lighthouse, for which he is most famed. Water and wind power were also of great interest to Smeaton, and after seven years' study of the subject his scientific experimentation and practical skills were acknowledged in 1759 by the Copley Medal – the Royal Society's most prestigious award.

Although much of Smeaton's time was spent at his four-storey retreat in Austhorpe Lodge near Leeds, the versatile independent engineer was no stranger to the North East

Chimney Mill's main sails and fantail were still intact in 1910, and are just visible in this view of North Terrace, part of Claremont Road. As Newcastle reached out to the suburbs, solid 'respectable' housing like North Terrace was extended to cater for the city's expanding middle class. Claremont Road was built in the late 19th century and its occupants included clerks, cashiers and a postmaster. *Newcastle City Library.*

North Terrace appears as comfortable with itself in the early 21st century as it was in the early 20th. All signs of more sedate forms of transport have gone and the foliage on the right has fortunately remained to screen the street from Newcastle's thundering Central motorway.

Windmill at Chimney Mill

and carried out site surveys for the reports he produced on Tyneside's harbours and docks as well as his commissions for dams on the Coquet and at Swalwell. During his career Smeaton is believed to have designed more than 50 watermills and six windmills, of which 'Chimney Mill' – built to replace an existing windmill at Spital Tongues in Newcastle – represented a significant technological advance.

Claimed to resemble the flared topcoat once worn by agricultural workers, the frock or 'smock' mill, as it became known, was a variant of the more common tower mill – built on a substantial masonry base – which was in use by the 13th century. In both types the sail cap could rotate independently to face the wind, and though the framework of the smock mill was made predominately of wood, Smeaton's structure on what became Claremont Road in Newcastle had distinctive new features to set it apart.

His windmill investigations led him to refine the construction of sails, and by introducing a cast-iron windshaft he brought the multi-sailed mill to Britain. Four sails were usually the norm, but five – reasoned to run more efficiently with increased power – were fitted by Smeaton to a Leeds flint mill in 1774 and to the Newcastle smock mill eight years later.

Yet, overall the weatherboarded mill appears to have been one of Smeaton's less successful projects. Fine in theory but flawed in practice, the 'Chimney Mill' pattern never became popular. Five sails may have rotated more aerodynamically, but the failure of one threw the windshaft off balance and corn milling ceased until the damaged sail could be repaired or replaced. In contrast, removing an opposite (and undamaged) sail from a six-sailed windmill returned it to service relatively quickly, so this model was more widely adopted.

Nevertheless, Smeaton's octagonal smock mill at Spital Tongues was wind-powered until 1891, when it was decommissioned and later used as a golf course clubhouse. After further conversions, and though long since shorn of cap and sails, this gleaming white structure – projecting above the rooftops on a busy city road – is Tyneside's salute to a great British engineer and a nostalgic reminder of a less frenetic age.

Despite the bold design of Newcastle University's campus, built a few hundred yards away after the establishment gained independence in 1963, Claremont Road is still highlighted by its oldest and simplest building. After conversion, the former 'smock' mill housed offices for a fashion design company and now accommodates the 'Windmill Dental Suite'.

28. South Street Locomotive Works, Newcastle

No 20 South Street, tucked away behind the grand architecture of Newcastle Central railway station, is a far plainer memorial to the Victorian age of steam. Two of its most significant engineers, George and Robert Stephenson, moved to the area in the 1820s and built locomotives that helped to change the world.

At the beginning of that decade, George Stephenson's career was entering a memorable phase. Following his work at Killingworth colliery, where he constructed and refined the locomotives *My Lord* and *Blucher*, his reputation had grown. It was enhanced by the building of an 8-mile waggonway from Hetton colliery to Sunderland, and consolidated by his appointment as chief engineer to the Stockton & Darlington Railway.

Land was obtained in Newcastle's Forth Banks district to support this major undertaking and a new company was formed. As well as involving iron master Michael Longridge, the business was managed by Robert Stephenson – then just 19, but aptly described as a 'rising star' of railway and civil engineering. The family partnership signalled the end of locomotive construction in makeshift workshops or colliery yards, and its South Street works, opened in 1823, became the world's first factory built specifically for locomotive manufacture.

Its first workshops were built on the east side of Newcastle's old upper town, but without the financial support of Quakers Thomas Richardson and Edward Pease they would never have got off the ground. Pease in particular – a wool trader – grasped the potential of George Stephenson's earlier work and was prepared to back it with his considerable wealth.

Within a few years his investment looked

In common with the surviving South Street buildings, archive images of the railway works are also hidden gems. This one taken in about 1950 from within the Central station complex gives a glimpse of the locomotive factory in its final guise as Robert Stephenson & Hawthorns Ltd. Behind loco No 67265 can be seen the top of a water tower built by the North Eastern Railway in 1897. Now Grade II listed, it had a capacity of 104,000 gallons. The locomotive is from Class 'G5', at that time allocated to Blaydon shed. The large signal gantry on the extreme right controlled departures from the station's west end. *Newcastle City Library*

South Street Locomotive Works, Newcastle

set to be repaid. *Hope*, *Black Diamond* and *Diligence* were all constructed at South Street, but it was *Locomotion* – the first engine built – that was universally recognised to be a success. George Stephenson was on the footplate of the reworked Killingworth design as it led a triumphal cavalcade at the inauguration of the Stockton & Darlington Railway in September 1825.

Unlike this snorting 'iron horse', however, the factory that produced it was somewhat slower to gather momentum. Ever ambitious, Stephenson senior had over-reached himself and, in the absence of his son in South America, accepted too many commissions and neglected his Newcastle base. A struggling South Street works had to be propped up by the loyalty (and hard cash) of its Quaker mentors until it was finally rescued by the return of Robert Stephenson, who afterwards became its driving force.

Under his renewed direction, the factory was given a great boost in 1829 with victory at the Rainhill Trials – a contest that in effect decided the future direction of locomotive technology. With its greatly improved boiler, Tyneside's legendary *Rocket* outperformed all comers, and its successors were soon in great demand. As railway mania took hold in the 1830s, the factory began to flourish, and South Street – with customers from America to Russia – became a locomotive manufacturer on a global scale. After Rainhill, the elder Stephenson was barely involved with engine design, but the business he had founded with his son moved on to become a major Tyneside employer. Following the death of Robert in 1859, the Forth Banks complex continued to be enlarged and over the next half-century offered a wide array of heavy engineering goods and services including stationary engines for colliery and marine use, railway wagon components and wrought-iron bridges.

Yet almost inevitably, lack of space forced Robert Stephenson & Company to

As business improved, Stephenson's factory was said to have 'absorbed' the remainder of South Street. Above the old factory door, an engine beam was used as a lintel, and the tall windows on the left brightened the boiler shops but, it was said, also turned them into a wintry 'Siberia'. Nevertheless, it is hoped that recent lease problems will soon be resolved and the Stephenson Trust's 'virtual' works tour can become a reality once more.

turn its back on Newcastle. A larger works was set up at Springfield in Darlington, and on 14 August 1902 the last in a line of more than 2,700 locos rolled from the South Street Works.

George and Robert Stephenson would have been fascinated by the motor cars and aeroplanes afterwards built on the site, and would have welcomed their modern successor, Robert Stephenson & Hawthorns Ltd, who returned to Forth Banks in 1937 to build locomotives for industrial railways. Manufacturing ended in 1960 and, thanks to the establishment of the Robert Stephenson Trust in 1988, sections of Stephenson's most hidden gem have now been saved and

Black and white engravings were the snapshots of the day, and this 1844 example from the *Penny Magazine*, published every Saturday, illustrates the interior of the Stephenson works. Equipment was basic and work practices hazardous to say the least. Before the installation of a works crane, heavy loads were manhandled with shear legs. Both George Stephenson's brother and brother-in-law were killed in factory accidents. *Newcastle City Library*

restored. Its mundane buildings lie beyond the railway tracks, bridges and embankments of a transport network the Stephensons did so much to make possible.

29. Hanover Street, Newcastle

After long periods of dereliction and demolition, Hanover Street is coming back to life. Now lined on its south side by smart apartment blocks, this hidden thoroughfare was a storehouse for Newcastle's river-borne trade.

A traffic warden appears ready to pounce on Hanover Street in 1965. The bonded warehouses of Amor Spoor are caught in the frame as a lorry-load of cases is readied near No 50. Spoor is recorded to have been a resident of nearby Clavering Place, and an entry in a directory of 1850 notes that Spoor & Son traded as 'bonecrushers'. Hemp, tallow and coffee were also stored in Spoors' warehouses. Stretching behind them is the King Edward VII Bridge. Opened in 1906, it was the last great railway bridge of Britain's age of steam. *Newcastle City Library*

Parking restrictions are even more rigorous in 2010, and judging by the lack of vehicles are remarkably successful. On the right, foliage spills over into Hanover Street and continues down the slope in an area known as the 'Hanging Gardens'. The superstructure across the background belongs to the Queen Elizabeth II Metro Bridge, completed in 1980.

Hanover Street and the Close were entering a spiral of decline when this photograph was taken in 1965. It shows the warehouse elevation on the Close, often compared to a towering cliff face. At that time a steep stairwell through the warehouses, currently not in use, connected Hanover Street to the Close below. *Newcastle City Library.*

It was on the waterfront that the town's commercial life got under way. During medieval times the quayside developed on both sides of the old stone bridge and a reclaimed strip of land to its west became the 'Close'. Jetties, staiths and warehouses were constructed on it, and from the prosperity earned by wool, hides and coal, merchants built timber-framed houses along what has been termed the 'Thames Street' of Newcastle.

In the 18th century, however, their residences began to be replaced by small industries and more warehousing as some of the town's wealthier citizens abandoned the river shore. They moved to less crowded

Hanover Street, Newcastle

Regeneration of the Close district began in the early 1990s with the Copthorne Hotel, built on a scale to match the tall warehouses opposite. In 2008 what remained of the bonded warehouses was integrated into a development of 134 apartments. Now rechristened 'Hanover Mill' (perhaps a reference to a steam-powered flour mill once in the vicinity), the rough and ready exterior brickwork of the restored building betrays a careworn past. The massive arched doorway of the former warehouse now leads to a Chinese restaurant.

and more fashionable districts inland and a century later businessman Amor Spoor appears to have followed the historic trend. An impressive range of buildings, erected for him between 1841 and 1844, extended down onto the Close. But they are known as the warehouses on Hanover Street, which was built a few years earlier to traverse the steep riverside slope and link the west end of the Quayside with the upper town.

Huge numerals once fixed on the building's Hanover Street façade indicated the purpose of Mr Spoor's new enterprise. The import and export trade required secure and readily identified storage for goods – mainly tobacco and alcohol – on which duty was deferred in exchange for bonds. 'Her Majesty's General Bond Warehouses' such as those opened on Hanover Street had been operational since 1803, when laws were passed to contain widespread excise evasion. With the introduction of authorised buildings and better-organised customs control, the Government was making it more difficult to evade the clutches of Britain's 'Revenue Men'.

Nevertheless, trade and warehousing always went hand in hand. The belated dredging of Newcastle Quayside during the mid-Victorian period helped the port to enjoy some of its busiest years, and consequently storage for an expanding stock of merchandise was required. Of the new warehouses built on the Close and along the riverbank to the east, the former CWS building, erected at the end of the 19th century, remains one of the most notable. Built to store cotton and grain and now a luxury hotel, the accomplished renovation of this massive reinforced concrete edifice was a keystone in the modern transformation of Newcastle's eastern quayside.

In comparison to this, the Hanover Street warehouses entered the 21st century in a far sorrier state. They were deserted in the 1970s and were subsequently wrecked by a series of fires. Now tastefully converted to apartments, only one – No 40 – of the five original bonded warehouses survives.

Yet for all this eventful history, Hanover Street's most hidden gem still sets it apart.

Forth Banks, in the first picture, and the approaches to the Swing Bridge were just two of many Tyneside slopes that benefited from inlaid cart tracks. This early transport aid is believed to have been an Italian system, introduced to Tyneside at the beginning of the early 19th century. *Newcastle City Library/Gateshead Library*

Parallel bands of smooth granite slabs curve away up the cobbled lane. Offset to the left for traffic on the sharp uphill slope, they were laid to assist traction for the ubiquitous horse and cart. Common enough before the reign of the internal combustion engine, few of Hanover Street's 'Stone Tramways' now remain.

30. Newcastle Swing Bridge

Newcastle and Gateshead Quayside is rightly celebrated for its many bridges. The Tyne Gorge is spanned by seven of them in a stretch of barely more than a mile. This dramatic bridgescape – a vibrant combination of old and new crossings – has come to embody both Tyneside's Victorian prowess and its growing confidence after years of industrial decline.

Indeed, the latest addition to the river scene has already become a modern icon. Driven by an ingenious tilting mechanism, the dual steel arches of the 850-tonne Millennium Bridge gracefully arc upwards to open for the passage of ships. Described recently as a 'perfect structure', the 2001 bridge is a mould-breaking concept acclaimed for its exhilarating modern design. Yet just upstream, the Swing Bridge was also a world-beater in its day. For more than a century, Newcastle's original opening bridge has maintained a low profile and, with the arrival of the streamlined newcomer, has slipped further from the public eye.

Believed to stand near the submerged piers of 'Pons Aelius' – a bridge built during the 2nd century of the Roman occupation – the Swing Bridge opened for traffic in 1876. It was perhaps fitting that the first large ship to pass through one of its open channels was an Italian naval transport bound for Armstrong's Elswick yard.

The crossing that the Swing Bridge replaced had become a major obstacle to the growth of the Tyne's riverborne trade. Almost from the start in 1781 Robert Mylne's nine-arched bridge – as classically elegant as it was – was found wanting. Even though proposals were made to widen and raise it, most agreed by the mid-19th century that the outmoded Georgian structure had become more of a barrier than a bridge. Businesses upstream were held back by it and many employers believed that they were held to ransom by the keelmen who skilfully negotiated their cargoes through its cramped arches.

Consequently, in 1864, after four years of often heated debate (including suggestions for a Tyne tunnel), work commenced. A temporary bridge was constructed and the Tyne Improvement Commission, which instigated the project, concluded its final plan and began to demolish the discredited old bridge. William Armstrong, whose business prospects were to greatly benefit from improved river access, was responsible for much of the advanced design of its replacement. His Elswick Works, a leading

Horse-drawn vehicles can be seen here observing the Highway Code at the Gateshead side of the Swing Bridge. While William Armstrong's factory was responsible for the wrought ironwork and machinery of the bridge, the Tyne Improvement Commission built the foundations. Assisted by Philip Messent, Chief Engineer John Ure designed and supervised the construction of three heavy granite piers. These were supported by cast-iron caissons, weighted with concrete and sunk into the riverbed. Thanks to the unseen work of these two forgotten men, the bridge has been able to operate smoothly for almost 150 years. *Newcastle City Library*

Swing Bridge traffic is more leisurely paced in August 2010. A stroll across the bridge is rewarded with splendid views of Newcastle's Norman keep and the crown-shaped tower of St Nicholas's cathedral church. High on the left is the combined High Level road and rail bridge; designed by Robert Stephenson with assistance from T. E. Harrison, it remains a masterpiece of cast and wrought iron engineering.

bridge manufacturer and within easy reach of the site, was perfectly placed to supply the wrought-iron superstructure and sophisticated hydraulics to power what was then to be the world's largest swing bridge.

Eight years in the building and delayed by a fire at Armstrong's factory, it was unceremoniously opened in June 1876, weighing in at 1,450 tons at a cost of almost £300,000. Armstrong's bridge swinging mechanism – an engineering masterpiece – is concealed in the bridge's heavy central pier. At its core is a ring of 42 cast-iron rollers supporting the road deck, which can be turned through a right-angle in a few minutes by two hydraulic engines. And crowning it all is a dainty cupola, from which a Bridge Master controls operations throughout the year.

At the official inauguration in July 1876, the bridge steadily pivoted like an Armstrong naval gun turret 'with marvellous smoothness and ease'. Since then it has continued to do so, with an estimated 300,000 vessels having slid through the bridge's 95-foot-wide river channels. Instead of a daily occurrence, however, bridge openings have now become something of a special occasion. Over the last few decades,

Because of the long exposure times once required in photography, static subjects were usually preferred. Yet this image has caught the Swing Bridge on the move. Looking downstream from the High Level bridge, it shows Armstrong's 281-foot-long structure about half-way through a 90-degree turn (a manoeuvre usually completed in an anticlockwise direction within a minute and a half). Taken in about 1910, the photograph shows a Newcastle-registered collier being towed by one of the river's resident paddle tugs – a common procedure during times of heavy river traffic. At its busiest in 1924 the bridge was opened for 6,000 vessels. Moored at the quayside on the left is a three-masted barque and other general cargo vessels, while on the Gateshead bank lies a wherry, one of the clinker-built cargo barges that succeeded the smaller keels. *Gateshead Library*

especially with the demise of the staiths beyond the bridge, river traffic has slowed to a trickle.

Yet though never the area's primary road transport route, the Swing Bridge has continued to earn its keep. Now almost lost in the crowd of majestic structures around it, the bridge remains a vital component of Newcastle and Gateshead's transport schemes. In the rush to work or to enjoy the attractions of a rejuvenated quayside zone, many pedestrians and motorists use this gem daily. William Armstrong's Swing Bridge has become one of his most valuable and enduring gifts to Tyneside.

Bridge 'swings' are rare occasions today, although pleasure craft have lately brought more business and in 2009 13 vessels passed through. Despite its significant initial contribution, by the 1920s the Tyne Improvement Commission reckoned that the job of the Swing Bridge was done and it should be demolished. Fortunately, the Commission's plan was never realised. Since then the bridge has become an industrial gem and, with the Tyne Road Bridge and the Millennium Bridge beyond that, a photographer's dream! Eye-catching modern architecture completes the scene. Dominating Gateshead quayside is a former flour mill, now the Baltic Centre for Contemporary Art, and at centre right is the much more controversially styled Sage Concert Hall.

31. Newcastle Brewery

As part of Tyneside's post-industrial fightback, Newcastle has been promoted as a new 'Party City' of the North. Yet well-earned leisure and entertainment have long been enjoyed in Newcastle, and its drinks industry has contributed greatly to this historic brew.

By the 19th century the ancient art of brewing was developing on an industrial scale. Beer in particular was a favourite beverage, often more wholesome than polluted town water and believed by some social commentators to be less dangerous to society than gin or even tea. Local centres of population soon developed significant beer-brewing industries, and Newcastle was no exception. By 1830 28 breweries were at work in Newcastle alone, producing beer claimed by contemporaries to be mostly 'strong' and consumed in 'prodigious' quantities. The Temperance Movement won some converts among the local working population, but as the century wore on beer's thirst-quenching properties became even more attractive to

Almost rivalling the giant war memorial, Newcastle Brewery's new offices figure prominently in the Haymarket in about 1905. Seen on the right, the ostentatious building contrasts sharply with the humdrum shops and houses it faces. When built, the neo-baroque building of red Dumfriesshire sandstone was described as one of the finest of its kind, with a basement equipped with strong rooms, wine cellars and the most up-to-date 'Plenium' system for heating and ventilation. *Newcastle City Library.*

Newcastle Brewery

Newcastle's expanding industrial army.

Taking advantage of new railway links, brewers from further afield moved to meet Tyneside's growing demand. Imports increased of 'superior' ales, but in 1884 a home-grown company began a business that brought better quality and wider appeal to Newcastle beer.

In that year, and after more than a century in Gateshead, brewer John Barras & Company left a successful but 'outdated' premises in Gateshead for the larger and well-equipped Tyne Brewery on

Even on a 'quiet' Sunday in July 2010 the Haymarket is one the city's most congested junctions. Overseen by the bronze figure of Victory, traffic squeezes past the recently reopened Metro station, rebuilt at a cost of £20 million. The Haymarket's sandstone war memorial was the work of local artist Thomas Eyre Macklin. The winged 'Victory' was removed and restored between 1975 and 1980.

Newcastle's Bath Lane, where brewing had been carried out since 1868. Under the direction of Charles Reed and benefiting from the expertise of Nottingham brewer and graduate chemist Thomas Lovibond, a series of popular local ales was produced, intended to improve the reputation and quality of Barras's beers. Then in 1889, to confirm the company's even greater ambitions, Barras became a public company, and a year later – further strengthened by amalgamation with four other regional companies – Newcastle Breweries Ltd was formed.

By centralising production in Newcastle, this large new company faced its challengers head on, and by 1900, after extensions to the Bath Lane plant, controlled more than 300 local pubs. For Thomas Lovibond, the transformation was complete and he

Frozen at moments almost half a century apart, these two portraits of the Tyneside Brewery's former headquarters are fortunate to exist. Taken in October 1964, the archive image suggests a bustling Percy Street and a handsome building in apparently good repair. However, cryptically written on the back of the photo is 'To be demolished'.

Today's photograph confirms that such a mistake was never made and the elevated road planned along Percy Street in 1963 remained on the drawing board. The brewery's old office complex is now Newcastle University's 'Bruce Building', named after John Bruce who founded the Percy Street Academy on the site in 1806. Among its distinguished pupils were Robert Stephenson and shipbuilder Charles Mark Palmer. *Newcastle City Library/Author*

Newcastle Brewery

Prince Charles declared St Thomas Street Workshops open in December 1986. Just off Percy Street, the former brewery stables now host a range of modern businesses, from financial consultants to record producers.

wrote that brewing (and by implication Newcastle Breweries) was at last 'worthy of a place' alongside the great industries of Victorian Tyneside.

Reflecting its rising status and confidence, the young brewery company built new headquarters on Percy Street in Newcastle's Haymarket, then a place where farm produce was still regularly traded. Ready for occupation in 1901, the new red sandstone and brick building was the Haymarket's architectural focus until 1907, when a towering Boer War obelisk was raised nearby.

Appropriately enough, the new office block was planted on a former brewery site, snapped up by the Tyneside Brewery in 1896 as part of a purchase from Sanderson's worth £206,000. Alongside the Percy Street frontage the company's acquisitive deal included a bonded warehouse on adjacent St Thomas Street, also once owned by John Sanderson & Sons, which had operated there since the 1850s. Redevelopment began at once and, when complete with mineral water and bottling factories, stabling for the heavy dray horses and the grand office suite, the 'magnificent' Haymarket complex marked a coming-of-age for Tyneside's newest and most important brewing empire.

From their mahogany-panelled boardroom on Percy Street, Tyneside Brewery's directors steered the company through decades of economic gloom, cheered somewhat by the introduction of the prize-winning bottled beer 'Newcastle Brown Ale' in 1927. A policy of business expansion and plant modernisation was slowed by the upheavals of war and 1950s austerity, yet extra bottling capacity and administration space was created at Bath Lane to compensate for the compulsory purchase of the Haymarket site. Although the brewery's loss was Newcastle University's gain, the Tyneside Brewery returned to its Bath Lane base with strengthened aspirations, and in 1960 merged with Scottish Brewers to join the top rank of British brewing.

But a long tradition was then entering a final phase. Scottish & Newcastle's decision to end brewing in Newcastle in 2005 and on Tyneside in 2010 was greeted with dismay. Hastily levelled, the extensive 19-acre Tyneside Brewery site is presently earmarked for development as an ambitious 'Science Park'. Now part of an international brewing giant, Scottish & Newcastle presently deliberates on its corporate affairs at a prestigious headquarters in Northampton, far from its northern heartlands. Yet 'Tyneside Brewery' remains carved above the company's old office door in Newcastle, and in neighbouring St Thomas Street visitors to the former brewery stable now walk across its cobbled yard.

Developments around St Thomas Street unfold beneath the camera in views separated by 46 years. Bonded warehouses at the lower right of the 1964 view are still recognisable in the modern photograph, and the 1840s buildings opposite have survived after considerate restoration in 1982. They are fine examples of a 'Tyneside Classical' style, influenced by John Dobson. Around them the towering University blocks approaching completion in 1964 are still being added to in the summer of 2010. *Newcastle City Library/Author*

32. New Bridge Street, Newcastle: Dobson's House and the Lying-in Hospital

John Dobson was Tyneside's premier architect, in Newcastle usually remembered for his Central station design and his association with Richard Grainger's majestic town plan. In 1854, after he had achieved success, Dobson stressed that he built mainly 'on a large scale', but in New Bridge Street, and remarkably within sight of each other, remain two smaller works from his earlier career.

John Stokoe's 'new bridge' was built in 1812 to cross the steep valley of the Pandon Burn – a stream that obstructed the eastern approaches to central Newcastle. The new bridge street was thus a convenient route into the heart of a town outgrowing its medieval boundaries, and as fashionable houses began to appear there it was an appropriate area for new architectural opportunities. Dobson quickly began to take advantage of them and

Because Newcastle's population almost quadrupled between 1841 and 1911, advertisers grabbed every opportunity to be noticed. But they had little respect for historic buildings in May 1911 when John Dobson's House was turned into a large billboard. After Dobson's death his New Bridge Street residence had been used as one of Henry Donnelly's lodging houses, and in 1925 became part of the Oxford Galleries, a popular dance hall. *Newcastle City Library*

The insomniac and teetotal architect may have disapproved of some New Bridge Street life in 2010. His former house has continued with the nightclub theme, rejoicing in such names as 'Tiffany's', the 'Ritzy', and lately 'Liquid' and 'Envy'.

What remains of New Bridge Street is now pedestrianised, but in 1965 it was still on the bus route. Tyneside Omnibus Company's No 51 (a Leyland Atlantean PDR1/1 with 75 seats) stands at the bus stop outside Dobson's Lying-in Hospital. In use as a hospital and refuge for the unemployed until 1923, the dilapidated building was repaired and converted for the BBC's Newcastle headquarters, transmitting radio and TV from there until 1988. *Newcastle City Library*

contributed to a 'rash of development', of which his own house, built in 1823, is now all that remains.

Born the son of a successful businessman at Chirton near North Shields in 1787, John Dobson remained faithful to his region and after an education in both Newcastle and London returned home to take up his chosen profession. At first based at Chirton, he moved his architect's practice to Pilgrim Street in Newcastle where he began to be offered more commissions. His first documented work for a private house was at Gateshead in 1813, followed by a decade where he modernised draughty old mansions and built new villas in an increasingly assured neo-classical style.

And though it is wedged between modern additions and heavily over-painted, the confident sophistication of Forty Nine New Bridge Street still shines through. As he did with larger houses, Dobson placed the entrance at the side, so as not to disturb the measured simplicity of the building's three-bay façade. Decoration is kept to a bare minimum and a delicate narrow frieze, its clay template crafted by Dobson himself, lies beneath a slender cornice. Although no trace remains of a lengthy garden used for the architect's collection of antiquities, Dobson's poised little home hints at a stylish area once featuring some of his best town houses, and was a prelude to Longhirst Hall outside Morpeth, built shortly afterwards in 1824 and in turn regarded as one of his finest country residences.

By this time Dobson was becoming a master of his art, doubtless commanding generous fees from a private clientele that included affluent members of Tyneside's increasingly numerous middle classes as well as the landed gentry. But his next building on New Bridge Street was a public work for which he made no charge.

Dobson's Lying-in Hospital, designed for Newcastle Corporation in 1825, is regarded by some experts as one of his less successful

New Bridge Street, Newcastle: Dobson's House and the Lying-in Hospital

architectural designs, but it was an early foray into the 'Tudor-Gothic' style and certainly served a useful social purpose.

The neat rectangular block replaced a house on the town's Rosemary Lane, used since 1760 as a maternity hospital for 'poor married women'. Funded by charitable subscription and donations, the new structure provided much improved facilities, catering for 12 patients. Erected by Messrs Welsh of Gateshead, the ashlar-faced new building backed onto the old town wall, and a contemporary engraving shows tall entrance pillars flanked by uninviting railings. Admission for expectant mothers was similarly forbidding. Pregnant women had to bring infants' clothing with them and a certificate of marriage, supported by a husband's sworn affidavit wherever possible.

Since then, both old-fashioned attitudes to pregnancy and the townscape of the New Bridge Street locality have undergone great change. Of fine public buildings, including a combined Library and Mechanics Institute, only an Edwardian art gallery remains. New Bridge Street is now truncated by a motorway scheme, created as part of utopian post-war planning to turn Newcastle into the 'Brasilia of the North'. Fortunately that strategy was never fully realised, but it did divert through traffic from an area lately reinvented as 'Blue Carpet Square', which contains Dobson's charming hospital and, opposite, the Georgian residence where he died in January 1865. For many years both buildings, but particularly his house, have found uses considered by some to be inappropriate. However, any purpose that at least respects the fabric of such historic buildings is surely better than none at all, and may have contributed to the welcome survival of this double share of Dobson gems.

After standing empty for several years, John Dobson's 'beautiful little building' was reopened as 'Portland House' in 1994. As part of the main office of a local building society, the former hospital still plays a public role. In this case its genial designer – remembered by the fishwives of Newcastle quayside as 'Cannie (sic) Mr Dobson' – would have approved wholeheartedly.

33. Carliol House, Newcastle

Newcastle's Carliol House on Pilgrim Street is often admired for its architectural quality, but less frequently considered is the great local industry that inspired its construction. Built as headquarters for the Newcastle Electric Supply Company, these monumental offices were erected between 1924 and 1927 after periods that witnessed a surge in the industrial, commercial and urban expansion of the area. The electrical power system developed to supply this growth was revolutionary on Tyneside and a blueprint for the rest of Britain.

At first, the provision of electrical energy was piecemeal and uncoordinated across the country, generally relying on the supply of low-voltage direct current over short distances to individual customers. This was sufficient for localised domestic lighting and tram services, for example, but it trailed behind the improving supply networks of economic competitors in Europe and the USA and was inadequate for an industrialising nation like Britain.

Nevertheless, Tyneside and the innovative engineers who worked there had played a dynamic part in the early history of electrical engineering. In 1880, shortly after the demonstration of Joseph Swan's domestic light bulb in Newcastle, Mosley Street became the first in Great Britain to be illuminated by electricity. Nine years later, but not far away on Shields Road in Heaton, a new factory constructed for internationally famed Charles Parsons built steam turbine generators that brought closer the dream of cheap and reliable electricity.

NESCo's flagship new building is pictured through a web of tram power cables in 1928. Clad in Portland stone, the steel-framed construction was named after the Carliol family of merchants who were early mayors of Newcastle. Constructed as a joint venture by London and Newcastle architects and builders, Carliol House was as innovative inside as out. As well as a cinema and lecture theatre, it included the latest built-in cleaning apparatus and had ultra-fast lifts (all electrically powered, of course). *Newcastle City Library*

Carliol House, Newcastle

But standing alongside these great engineering luminaries, the groundbreaking work of Newcastle's Electric Supply Company – energised by the major contribution of the less well-recalled Charles Merz – helped as much to create today's modern world.

Founded in 1889 to exploit exciting new opportunities of electrification on Tyneside, the Newcastle-upon-Tyne Electric Supply Company (known as 'NESCo') went on to become the prime mover in power generation and distribution across the region. Initially sharing the Newcastle territory with Parson's District Electricity Lighting Company, NESCo eventually gained the upper hand after recruiting Charles Merz as its Chief Consultant Engineer.

The first major project of Charles Hesterman Merz, born in Gateshead in 1874, could not have been more technologically significant. In 1899 the young engineer began the design of a power station that signalled a victory in what has been termed 'the battle of the systems'. The result of his work was unveiled in 1901 at Wallsend when Neptune Bank became the first coal-fired power station in Britain to generate three-phase alternating current. Building on the work of scientist Nikola Tesla and American engineer George Westinghouse, Merz and his collaborator William McClellan began to break free from small-scale generating operations that had restricted the progress of electrification, to design high-voltage power systems that set the pattern for generations to come.

Through the early decades of the 20th century, NESCo – with Scotsman McClellan increasingly at its core – extended its reach across the North East. Carville in Wallsend, built in 1903 mainly for the electrification of the North Eastern Railway's coastal line, was extended to become the most economical power station in the world, and was followed by others including Blaydon Burn, North Tees and Dunston 'B'. Reminiscent of the waggonways and rail networks before it, this Tyneside company and its brilliant masterminds began to sketch out the first lines of what would become a National Grid.

Expanding from its Newcastle base, NESCo evolved to become the North East Electrical Company in 1932 and its headquarters, after years as a saleroom for the local Electricity Board, became a retail and office complex that fittingly included an energy firm. But the Portland-stone-clad Carliol House remains to symbolise the soaring early success of NESCo on Tyneside. Rising above the corner of Market Street and Northumberland Street like a majestic white ocean liner, it was built to celebrate a brave and bright new world.

Now adrift from Newcastle's main shopping area, this part of Pilgrim Street awaits a face-lift. Carliol House's neighbour on the left has been condemned for its 'sheer ugliness', and redevelopment of this so-called Newcastle 'Gateway' is due to commence shortly. Carliol House is tipped to become a luxury hotel, but whatever the outcome this hidden gem will always be one of the city's best architectural assets.

34. Keelman's Hospital, Newcastle

The Keelman's Hospital in Newcastle is a handsome building that keeps alive the fading memories of a lost trade and the communal way of life that depended upon it. This gem stands proudly above Newcastle City Road to the east of the old city wall and looks out to the river where the town's famed boatmen once plied their trade. The hospital was built in 1701 in Sandgate, originally a quayside suburb of the medieval town. As the medieval era ended and coal

Almost two centuries of grime had already coated the Keelman's Hospital when this image of Newcastle's New Road was made. A few years later, in 1883, the thoroughfare was renamed City Road to celebrate Newcastle's official designation as a city. Next to the hospital on the right is the Royal Jubilee School, opened in 1810 for elementary education of poor children. This was John Dobson's first major design – an astonishing classical temple, now demolished. In the distant haze are Newcastle's Castle keep, the Cathedral of St Nicholas and the 195-foot spire of All Saints church. *Newcastle City Library.*

The Keelman's Hospital has stepped from the shadows in 2010. A spruced-up façade has reaffirmed it as a significant Georgian survival – one of a trio in Newcastle built predominantly of brick. It is reached from the Quayside via Sandgate Steps, in an area once unflatteringly known as 'Lousy Hill'. John Wesley preached around there in 1742. A plan of the hospital from 1722 shows that it originally had two towers.

and shipping began to prosper, Sandgate too began to grow and became a densely populated district later described as the 'Wapping of Newcastle'.

But this bustling enclave was also the keelman's stronghold. Sandgate's narrow streets were home to this group of independent-minded workers who first surfaced in the public records as 'kelers' in 1378. The vessel that earned them their living was a traditional northern craft

– about 40 feet long, 20 feet beam, flat-bottomed and of shallow draught, and able to carry about 20 tons of coal piled into its hull. A single square sail could be hoisted, but generally the keel was more barge than sailing boat and is said to have been a clumsy vessel, until steered by the keelmen, who were held to be 'the finest sailors and handlers of craft in England'.

Much of the imagery surrounding this clan of Tyneside boatmen is similarly high flown. Elements of it, however, in particular the keelmen's reportedly colourful 'uniform' – including silk black headgear and yellow waistcoats – have been dismissed by a recent popular writer as Victorian whimsy. Nevertheless, it seems certain that from an early date the keelmen formed a distinct group, aware of their own separate identity and able to organise collective action, usually in response to threats against their wages and conditions.

References to a Keelman's Craft Fraternity appear in 1539, and some of its more prosperous members, able to buy their own boats and houses, certainly displayed a measure of real independence. About a century later, the keelmen were employed by Newcastle's Hostmen or 'fitters' – the cartel of middlemen who exerted a powerful

Sandgate and the Keelman's Hospital are framed within the 164-foot-high arch of the Millennium Bridge. Just to the right is the former CWS warehouse, now a luxury hotel and one of Britain's first large ferro-concrete structures.

hold on Tyneside's coal trade. Once afloat, however, the keelman was again his own master, subject only to the vagaries of weather and tide.

Indeed, it is easily forgotten that the tidal reaches of the river, now for the most part a deep and well regulated waterway, were once impeded by shallows and sand banks. Before the Tyne Improvement Commission finally began work in the mid-19th century, even the harbour mouth at South Shields was at times barely passable. After paying to be piloted past its sand bars and rocks, ships under sail had sometimes then to endure a two-week voyage before docking at Newcastle Quay, only 12 miles upstream. Yet in these early days of the coal trade it was here that the keelmen's rivercraft skills gave them the upper hand. Tyne watermen were long experienced in punting, rowing and sailing their keels through difficult stretches of a dangerous river. After embarking on the ebb tide with their cargo, the keels went alongside much larger colliers anchored in deeper water offshore or at Tynemouth's 'Natural Dock'. Coal was then shovelled up to the collier's deck high above the keelmen's heads – a laborious task, often accomplished in darkness, which added to the keelman folklore. R. J. Charleton's much-quoted history of Newcastle typically describes them as a 'hardy and athletic body of men'.

But accounts of their unity against authority have contributed most of all to the keelman legend. An attempt to collect a Hearth Tax in Sandgate sparked off a riot in 1666, and over the next century the keelmen cemented their reputation for unruly dissent. By the early 19th century they were in the vanguard of industrial unrest as they struck against wage reductions and the proliferation of coal spouts and staiths. Since their introduction, the river boatmen generally resented these wooden contraptions, but they reserved their greatest contempt for spouts that poured coal directly into ships and brought unemployment to keelmen 'below the bridge'. In a dispute that rumbled on and culminated in the ten-week 'long stop' strike of 1822, keelmen fought with police and were shot at by Marines, but ultimately could not resist the march of technology. *Wylam Dilly* was the shape of things to come – on water as well as land. Converted into a steam paddle tug, William Hedley's locomotive engine towed a line of keels downstream to break the strike.

Economic power had slipped from the keelmen's grasp and they returned to work with dignity but with no concessions won. Unexpectedly, where most contemporary sources condemn them, the Duke of Northumberland praised the keelmen's final great protest for its relative moderation.

But they would never again be a force to be reckoned with, and although they maintained relatively high wages and employment levels from collieries to the west of Newcastle, their centuries-old trade was dealt a mortal blow by the construction of the Swing Bridge in the late 1860s and the dredging of the river channels that followed.

Continued funding of their hospital was always dear to the keelmen's hearts and often at issue during industrial disputes. Erected at the keelmen's expense for their old and infirm, the two-storey building was later owned by Newcastle Corporation, and by the mid-20th century was the home of caretaker 'Old Geordie Tulip', who claimed to be the last of the keelmen. Like him, the keelboat had become just as rare. For a few years some splintered keel wrecks lingered on at the water's edge, swamped by the wake of the Tyne wherries and steam colliers that had replaced them.

Yet the old two-storey hospital remains. Although standing back from Newcastle's gleaming new quayscape, its white entrance bay is a striking memorial to the keelmen. In 1885 they were portrayed by writer and amateur historian William Tomlinson as a 'nearly extinct race'. Could he now visit a bustling Quayside on a Saturday night, alive with the latest generation of ebullient young Tynesiders, he might change his mind.

A Tyneside keel, seen through the eyes of a 21st-century artist. An apprentice known intriguingly as a 'peedee' assisted the keel skipper and his two-man crew.

35. Ouseburn: the Maling Pottery

Tyneside was famed for ceramics as well as ships. What was claimed to be the largest pottery factory in Britain, if not the world, is now 'Hoult's Yard', a cleverly restored range of old work buildings and new office space in the Ouseburn area to the east of Newcastle's city centre.

The Ouseburn – longest and last of Newcastle's ancient streams now not entirely buried underground – flows 9 miles from the suburbs of Newcastle to its outlet at the Tyne. Beyond the perimeter of the old city walls, the lower Ouseburn valley became a ballast shore and during its hectic industrial phase was overlain with a wide range of industries including pottery manufacturers, active in the area since the late 18th century.

Robert and John Maling joined them in 1815, transferring to Newcastle an already established Sunderland business that had been set up by their grandfather, William Maling, from the proceeds of his coal, timber and shipping fortune. Originally of Huguenot stock, his family were among the many refugees from religious persecution to stamp their 'mark of excellence' on Tyneside's skilled craft trades.

Access to the sea and European customers was an important factor in the Maling relocation. And the availability of earthenware ingredients – flint, white and brown clay and glazing materials, all fired by cheap local coal – made Tyneside and the Ouseburn the ideal location.

Operational from June 1817, the Ouseburn Bridge kilns were prosperous enough for the firm to later acquire a neighbouring pottery, but under the ambitious leadership of a new owner Maling's was driven to its greatest success. An outstanding Victorian entrepreneur, Christopher Maling effected dramatic change to the company with a new and much larger Ouseburn factory, opened in 1859. Ambitious and competitive, with a keen business eye, he introduced automation wherever possible, adopting steam-powered technology. This allowed him to step up production, especially of food pots, and embrace a utilitarian mass market that would mould Maling's prosperity for the next half-century.

Known by his wife's family name, Maling's

An advertising poster from the 1929 Newcastle Exhibition presents a bird's-eye view of the extensive Ford 'B' Pottery. Aimed to boost Tyneside's ailing trade and industry, the Exhibition's six-month spectacle drew in more than 4 million visitors to the Town Moor site. Unlike some fellow exhibitors at that time, however, the Maling business was in relatively good shape. This was due in no small part to their respected London agent, Mr S. Stanley, who for 25 years until his death in 1935 maintained Maling's high profile, particularly in a keenly contested home market. Newcastle City Library

Even though scaffolding shrouds the interior entrance to Hoults, the photographer did not need to move beyond the railway bridge for this 1965 image of the former Maling works. By then ceramic production was finished at the old Ford Pottery, but Hoults – established by Edward Hoult in 1917 on Newcastle's Bridge Street – was well on its way to becoming a leading removal and storage firm on Tyneside and in Britain. *Newcastle City Library*

Apart from foreign models replacing British cars, little appears to have changed in what is now called 'Hoults Yard'. The row of buildings on the left was Maling's main manufacturing area where mystifying pottery operations such as 'casting, dipping and jollying' were carried out. Happily the site was retained for enterprise units and is now directed by new Hoult family entrepreneurs.

brand new 'Ford Pottery' far outstripped the output of any predecessor. Thirteen kilns and their allied machinery gave the new works a capacity of 750,000 finished articles per month – a startling volume that was nevertheless soon eclipsed. In 1879, half a mile from what was then termed Ford 'A', an even larger Ford 'B' factory took shape. Costing £100,000, on a 14-acre site, the new complex was a model of integrated manufacturing. Tons of flint was crushed at the beginning of the process and huge numbers of pots would emerge at the end to be loaded at nearby quayside wharves or transported from the factory's internal railway sidings. Output was claimed to have doubled across the Ouseburn sites, which towards the end of the century employed more than 1,000 workers, many of them women. Indeed, the use of lead-free glazes in comparatively airy and bright new workshops was believed to have attracted more skilled labour, among them potters from Staffordshire, then at the centre of Britain's earthenware manufacturing. This was a time of increasing demand when a majority of Victorian consumers spread their jam or spooned beef extract from pottery jars made at Maling's Ouseburn works.

Christopher Thompson Maling died in 1901, leaving three sons who were already proving themselves worthy successors. They are credited with broadening the commercial appeal of the company, rebranded as C. T.

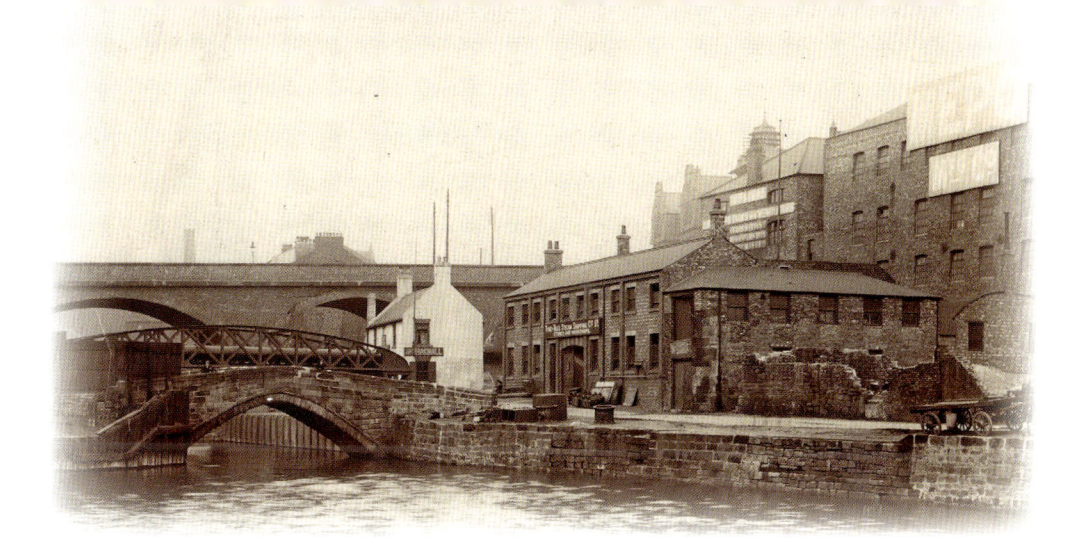

Maling & Sons in 1889. Diversification came in the form of wider ranges of decorated pottery – most notably the predominantly white 'Cetem Ware', then, in the 'roaring' 1920s, a more stylish and colourful Maling lustre ware. Many were designed by renowned painter Lucien Boullemier and, with their distinctive castellated trademark, proved popular then and are widely collected today.

Yet, despite surviving the closure of Ford 'A' during the General Strike and the trading difficulties of the following decade, Maling's ultimately became a victim of its own long-established success.

As competition resumed in the post-war period, Maling's began to fail. Skill shortages worsened the situation, but worst

Only two years away from demolition, Ouseburn's early Glasshouse Bridge is captured for posterity in this 1906 image. Denoting the valley's first major industry, the single-arched bridge replaced an older wooden structure, which had been rebuilt in stone by shipwright Thomas Wrangham in 1669. *Newcastle City Library*

Ouseburn's industry has come and gone since the era of the ancient Glasshouse Bridge. The latest footbridge has been comprehensively autographed by graffiti 'artists', but the high-level road viaduct, built in 1878, is less easily marked. In front of it, the £4.7 million Ouseburn Barrage lifts its concrete and steel head, while on the right the old Ship Tavern, now the Tyne Bar, has been described as 'Newcastle's best-kept secret'. Above them all, however, are the unmistakable pagoda-style towers of Ouseburn Schools, built between 1891 and 1893 and now a business centre.

of all was overproduction and the lack of investment in what had became an outdated factory. Condemned for making 'far too many articles', it was rescued in 1948 by Hoults, an ambitious local furniture removal firm that did all it could to revive the Maling heritage on Tyneside. However, they could not stave off the industry's national decline. Despite the installation of new equipment and the imposition of tighter product control, crucial orders were lost to Far East rivals, and in 1963 the Ford Pottery shut down.

Maling's old clock tower, now a café, was once the factory's Fire Station.

36. Wills cigarette factory, Heaton

The stylish Wills Building in Heaton on Newcastle's Coast Road was built for a far less fashionable use. It began life as a cigarette factory in 1946, but had been planned years before in the severe 1930s downturn when unemployment overshadowed health as the burning social issue of the day. At that time – contrary to popular belief – not every

W. D. & H. O. Wills's best-selling brand names are on display in this 1967 photograph of its High Heaton factory. Roadworks are progressing on the Coast Road, a main arterial route that, like the Wills building, was a 1930s design, and was rebuilt in the late 1960s. In some of its advertising, Wills's claimed that it was 'delivering the goods by road'. *Newcastle City Library*

Wills cigarette factory, Heaton

sector of the economy was affected, but much of Tyneside's traditional heavy industries were hit hard. In 1934 the Government responded with financial assistance, and while the City of Newcastle was not included, Tyneside was designated as one of Britain's 'Special Areas' of need. Two years later, and costing £2 million, Gateshead's Team Valley Trading Estate, eventually home to scores of businesses, shops and a hotel, began to take shape. Yet the success of Tyneside's most extensive industrial park – its wide tree-lined main avenue stretching for 2 miles – was frustratingly slow. During the pre-war period, although the number fell far short of official expectations, more than 2,500 jobs were created. But also held out was a new vision of industry, where progressive employers could provide lighter and cleaner jobs (many of them for women) in a safe manufacturing environment. W. D. & H. O. Wills seemed to match these criteria when it decided to manufacture cigarettes in suburban Newcastle. The famous company, based in Bristol, was long established in the tobacco trade, producing household names like 'Gold Flake' and 'Woodbine' cigarettes. As part of the Imperial Tobacco Company, it had achieved international status, but retained a family firm reputation as a considerate employer.

Although delayed by the intervention of war and four years in construction, the factory was finally declared open in 1950. Designed by Cecil Hockin, Imperial Tobacco's resident architect, the steel-framed building was reported to be 'spacious, light and airy' and, together with its monumental office frontage, owed much to American influences of layout and style. Subsidised by post-war Development Area grants, the new structure also appeared to represent taxpayers' money well spent. Certainly the company scored an early success in public relations. As well as providing enviable employee facilities, it hosted regular works tours, which were a popular attraction for years to come.

Cigarette-making, carried out in the large factory space behind the office block, also proceeded smoothly. After initially relying on skilled workers from Bristol, the local workforce 'learned the ropes' and, though never immune to labour disputes, contributed to Imperial Tobacco's continued growth and diversification. Towards the end of the 1970s the Newcastle factory was experiencing a 'king size' boom, and a new night shift clocked on to deal with the huge demand for a new product brand. At Heaton's peak – with a workforce exceeding 1,000 – more than 200 million cigarettes shuttled weekly from Wills's increasingly sophisticated machinery and a similar number were held in the factory's own bonded store.

Road signs now proliferate outside the former cigarette factory. Although the manufacturing area was demolished, subsequent alterations have not been allowed to spoil its much-praised red brick and Portland stone façade. Now known as the Wills Building, this popular location has become a hot property for local estate agents. In 1986 one of them argued that the empty building was unsaleable and should be knocked down.

But significant problems were mounting up for the tobacco giant. Always subject to intense competition and price rises in tobacco duty, the industry was also losing the heated argument about tobacco-related diseases. Cigarette sales in Western Europe began to fall and, despite reorganisation and the introduction of new equipment at Heaton, Imperial Tobacco closed the Coast Road factory in 1986.

The decision was met with genuine sadness by many of its employees. Redundancy or relocation of some workers to distant parts of the country was poor recompense for the majority of the workforce in a declining jobs market. Attempts by cigarette lighter firm Ronson to transform the site into a business centre were rejected by Imperial Tobacco, and the factory lay empty through the next decade – deteriorating and prone to vandalism. Eventually, but at the cost of demolishing the rear factory area, the threatened structure was rescued by property developer George Wimpey plc and fitted out with 114 apartments. Although its working life was relatively short, Hockin's art deco gem suited its new purpose admirably and demonstrates the versatility and resilience of well-thought-out industrial architecture.

37. Wallsend Colliery

In this postcard view from the early 20th century, Wallsend's Roman fort is just out of frame on the left while Buddle Street leads to the site of 'B' pit. By that time, similar terraced rows covered much Roman archaeology, but the shallow foundations of workers' housing left the remains of Segedunum largely undisturbed. The photograph features Wallsend's decorative public clock, believed to have been placed there by Swan Hunter & Wigham Richardson Ltd, which owned the shipyard opposite. *North Tyneside Libraries (North Shields).*

Road widening led to a move fo the Grade II-listed timepiece, and it now stands at the gates o Swan Hunter's empty shipyard. After more than 130 years, the Wallsend yard lost its last battl against closure and in June 201 the framework of Swan's last two cranes came crashing down New industrial giants are set to rise from the wreckage, howeve Factories to manufacture giant wind turbine blades and wire ro have been built at the old Nept yard, next to Wallsend's most famous shipbuilding berths.

Wallsend Colliery

While forever connected with Hadrian's great stone frontier, the town of Wallsend is built over a more ancient and deeply hidden wall. More than 600 feet below the surface and about 6 feet high, the 'High Main' was the most accessible of several coal seams that lay beneath the riverside district. Domestic coal from it was highly prized and became a benchmark for quality across the trade. When the 'A' pit of financier and mine-owner William Russell finally reached this rich seam in 1781, the development of modern Wallsend effectively began.

Six other shafts followed in the next quarter of a century, dotted around the area and given the usual alphabetical designations. First among them was 'B' pit, sunk across the course of Hadrian's Wall and near the foundations of Wallsend's long-abandoned Roman fortress of 'Segedunum' (usually translated to mean 'strong' or 'victory fort'). By the mid-18th century Wallsend had been little more than 'a very delightful village' north of the former military garrison. In the 19th century, however, a less hostile population influx began and as Wallsend's mineshafts went deeper its expanding workforce began to suffer the consequences of the quest for coal.

In 1808, although Wallsend's new pits topped the league table for coal sales on Tyneside, they also began to set grimmer records. Because the High Main reserves were being worked out, attention was switched to the deeper and more dangerous 'Bensham' seam. Mine engineer John Buddle described it to be 'particularly fiery' and, indeed, the 52 fatalities brought about by an explosion in this 'gassy' seam in 1821 was only a tragic prelude to a worse disaster.

Wallsend's 'G' pit exploded again on the afternoon of 18 June 1835, this time causing the death of 102 boys and men aged between 8 and 76. Often known as 'Church Pit' because of its proximity to St Peter's parish church, the mine was badly damaged and almost half the total workforce killed. It was a calamity that the expertise of John Buddle, one of the North East coalfields' longest-serving colliery 'viewers', seemed powerless to prevent. During the inquest he stoutly defended both his complex 'air splitting' method of ventilation and the superiority of Humphrey Davy's safety lamp, which he preferred to George Stephenson's home-grown version. A convinced jury found no one to blame for an accident that Coroner Stephen Reed declared would 'remain a mystery for ever'.

As well as a lifetime association with Wallsend, John Buddle junior also advised coal-owners on all aspects of mining activity and planned and managed collieries on their behalf. During this early period Buddle was a leading member of an emerging 'viewing' profession. He was a specialist in the 'black arts' of mining who became highly influential and respected in the coal trade and reaped its considerable financial rewards. At his death in 1843 he had amassed a sizeable fortune and, like him, many other viewers mixed their 'independent' consultation work with colliery ownership, setting up conflicting interests between safety and profit for which they attracted fair criticism at the time. Some of this continues to be levelled at John Buddle, but while it is certainly difficult to accept him as the so-called 'patron saint' of underground ventilation, he was an advocate of accident prevention in coal mines and made valuable contributions to the development of early mining and coal transport engineering.

After his death, however, it was not inadequate ventilation but another ever-

Wallsend's four-faced cast-iron clock is believed to have been manufactured by Gillott & Johnson of Croydon in the late 19th century. They made a similarly styled Gothic clock for the Mayor of Gateshead in 1892.

present danger that helped to close Buddle's home pit. With the exhaustion of the High Main seam and the withdrawal from service of the mighty pumping station upstream at Friar's Goose, water flooded most of the Mid-Tyne collieries. Production ceased at Wallsend in 1854 and was not resumed until 1897, when a new pit was sunk and the deadly Church Pit was briefly raised back to life.

Over the following decade, Wallsend's era of coal-mining entered a concluding phase with the opening of the 'Rising Sun' colliery, named after a farm on the town's northern edge. Employing up to 2,000 workers, it became one of Tyneside's largest and most successful mining operations and, when closed amidst a chorus of protest in 1969, was the last working pit on the Tyne's north bank. Yet even though achieving a respectable safety reputation, this last Wallsend colliery could never shake free from its stealthy old enemy. Exploding methane gas killed five miners in 1925 and, a few years before closure, the fatal 'G' pit – then being used to pump water – claimed a final victim.

Four hundred acres of 'natural green oasis' have now replaced the Rising Sun, and while Wallsend commemorates its 1835 pit casualties with one small churchyard plaque, Buddle's name is very evident around the town. He died there in 1843 and is recalled by an Industrial Estate, Arts Centre and road. Nevertheless, consolidated scraps of brickwork from 'B' pit can be seen at the end of Buddle Street opposite the Roman fort. Visitors walk past original boiler room walls to climb a modern reconstruction of Emperor's Hadrian's famous Wall. From its high rampart they can reflect on the 'glory' that was Rome and look across to Wallsend's lowest-profile industrial gem.

> Probably because they were enclosed in a builder's yard, the skeletal outlines of Wallsend's Roman Wall and Buddle's 'B' pit have survived side by side. Both are now exposed and a section of 'new' Wall – erected between 1993 and 1996 at a height of 12 feet – looms over the lower courses of its ancient predecessor. Amongst 'B' pit's jumble of stonework is a capped-off shaft that was used to ventilate surrounding workings after the mine closed in 1847.

38. Willington Ropery

Before embarking on their celebrated careers, George Stephenson and his young son Robert briefly lived at Willington Quay, near Wallsend. But the achievements of another family of engineers who stayed much longer at Willington are now largely forgotten. William and Edward Chapman established a ropery there in 1789, and more than 200 years later Willington remains a significant centre of British

When this photograph was taken the ropeworks of Hood, Haggie & Son was 'amongst the largest and finest in the country'. Several hundred people were employed by Haggie's including their renowned 'Angels', some of whom began work at the age of 14. The tallest of these girls were selected to work with hemp, which was difficult to handle and said to produce clouds of green dust. A much earlier employee was claimed to be George Stephenson, who is believed to have maintained the engine at the ropeworks for a few weeks at the beginning of the 19th century. *North Tyneside Libraries (North Shields)*

Once filled with Haggie's quarter-mile-long ropewalk, Willington Dene would now make a fine 'heritage trail'. Little remains to detract from the spectacular viaduct – itself a gem – which was built by local engineers John and Benjamin Green. Noteworthy for its time, the viaduct's original arches were made from laminated timber.

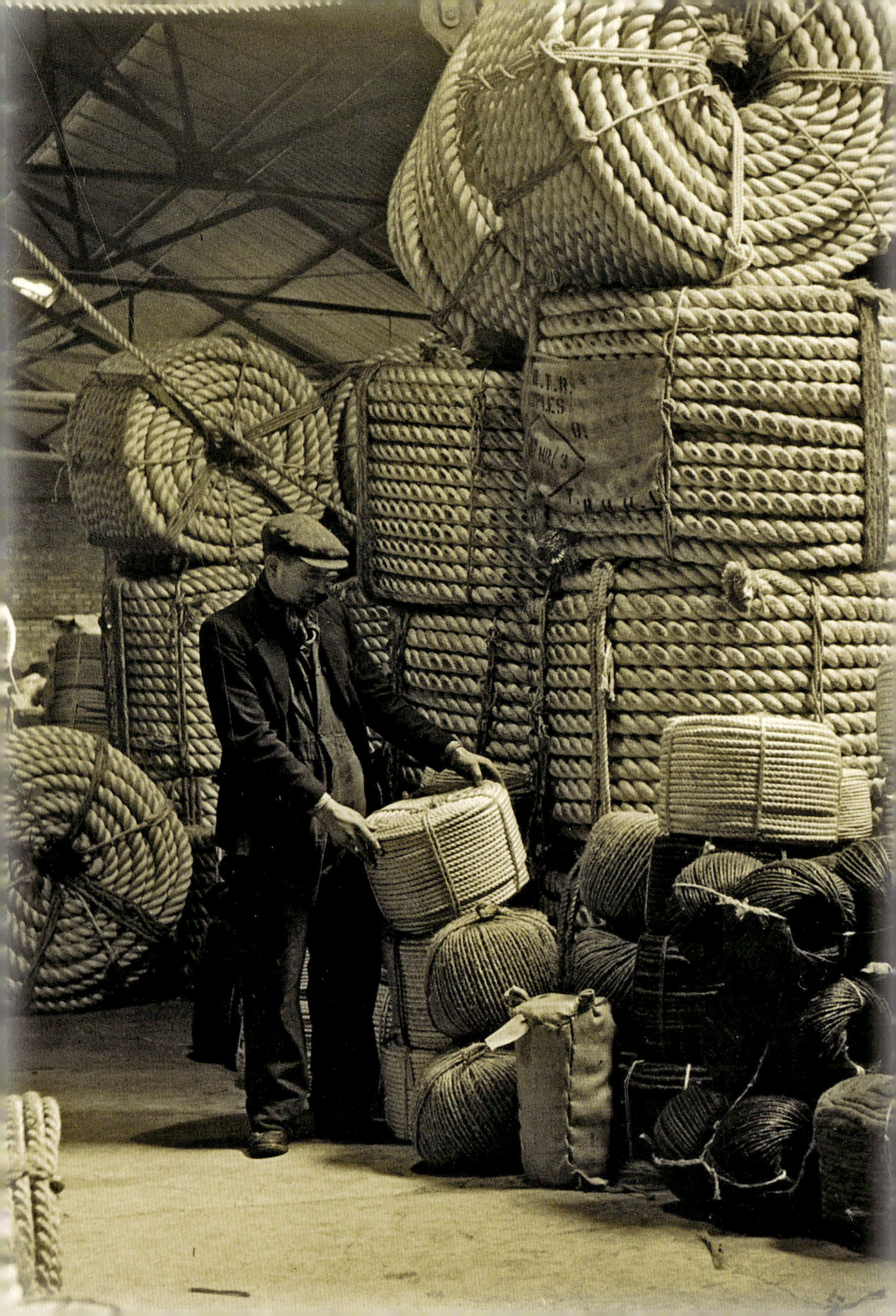

Willington Ropery

rope manufacturing.

For centuries, rope was the sinew of Britain's maritime and industrial history. The Age of Sail in particular would have been impossible without it, and Tyneside, like other port areas, had several local rope-makers. The framework of an open-air 'ropewalk' – where workers paced backwards with bundles of hemp or sisal wrapped around their waist – is clearly visible on an early-18th-century map of Newcastle. Some long walks were roofed over and an element of mechanisation was introduced, but even then rope continued to be turned out in a largely traditional way. Straightened lengths of yarn were laid out on the ropewalk, then twisted together by a group of rotating hooks. The other yarn ends were fixed to a single hook on a trolley or 'sledge', which was then pulled down the walk, binding the strands into a tightly woven rope.

In the late 18th century, a minimum of 720 feet of tarred rope was required to anchor a typical Admiralty vessel. It has been estimated that to sail into battle, a fully rigged naval 'first rater' required 42 miles of line weighing almost 80 tons. It followed then that Britain's conflicts abroad and industrial revolution at home would only increase the demand for rope and encourage the building of factories such as Willington.

Before the ascendancy of industry, this small village was 'a little Arcadia'. But its tranquillity had been disturbed by one of North Tyneside's earliest waggonways even before Chapman's ropery began production. 'The Willington Patent Ropery', as it was first known, was built in a scenic valley on the tidal Willington burn, which flows to the adjacent river quay. Bulky hemp bales could be delivered by keel to the warehouse, then to the workshop where raw fibre, usually lubricated with whale oil, was hand combed through metal spikes or 'hatchels' in preparation for spinning. But the innovation of William and Edward Walton Chapman greatly improved various time-honoured processes of the finished rope.

After the death of their father in 1793, the Chapman brothers, originally from a family of Whitby seafarers and ship-owners, took full charge of the Willington enterprise and enlarged it. Of the brothers, Edward was the 'practical rope maker' who lived on site and managed the works. It was a combination of his ability and his older brother's wider engineering talents that distinguished their new Tyneside factory, making it 'the most perfect of the kind in England', as the 5-acre Willington site was later described.

William Chapman in particular has never been given the recognition he deserves. Not only did the former sea captain patent advanced rope-making machines and write a treatise on rope manufacture, but his contribution to early railway and coal transport design has also been largely underestimated. Nevertheless, his inventions certainly helped to set the Willington Ropery on the road to success. One of them, called 'The Waltzer', produced rope of 'endless length' and operated for more than a century.

Although much of the original works was burned down in 1873, it was rebuilt around a surviving ropewalk that was retained for certain processes. The new rope works eventually covered 15 acres and the name of its owners went on to become synonymous with rope production, both on Tyneside and across an international trade. Just over 20 years later a 5-ton manila towing cable, produced at Willington by R. Hood, Haggie & Sons, was the largest ever made. And in more recent times the name of 'Haggie's Angels' – Willington's hard-working and independent female employees – has passed into local folklore.

Despite difficult periods for its factories on Tyneside and on Wearside, particularly during the 20th century, the company has survived. Maintaining the policy of its founders, new machines were brought in and new techniques implemented at Willington. Over time, a changing market called for more 'flexible' steel wire rope and 'binder twine', then rope made from modern,

This photograph from about 1946, almost certainly of Willington Ropery, shows the variety of ropes produced there. North Tyneside Libraries (North Shields).

much tougher synthetic materials such as nylon. Post-war reconstruction took place in response to this before the Willington plant was incorporated into British Ropes in 1959. Afterwards it became part of Bridon International Ropes, and since then the Willington Quay factory has become Bridon's British flagship.

Now demolished, Willington's old ropery site is turning back into a little country walk. Yet on the side of the burn just to the south, its modern successor turns out 20,000 tons of industrial rope yearly using the latest sophisticated machinery. Hopefully this 'high tech' gem can anticipate a future as long as one of William Chapman's endless ropes.

Completed in 1839 for the Newcastle & North Shields Railway Company, Willington Viaduct now serves as a vital component of the Metro, Tyneside's rapid transit rail system.

Pictured through a viaduct arch in 2009, Bridon Ropes holds the line for Willington's historic rope-making tradition.

39. Howdon Pedestrian Tunnel

At a time when the newest Tyne Tunnel has just been completed, one of the oldest is becoming even more of a hidden gem. Opened for pedestrians and cyclists in 1951, the submerged link from Howdon to Jarrow was the realisation of much earlier plans.

In 1797 local engineer Ralph Dodd proposed a 14-foot-diameter 'dry tunnel' between North and South Shields, reducing an overland journey of 18 miles to a few hundred yards. Although a similar suggestion was made to replace Newcastle's near-obsolete Georgian bridge in 1864, and other cross-river schemes were aired in the early 20th century, it was not until after the Second World War that real progress was seen.

On 4 June 1947, a year after Parliament approved the construction of pedestrian and cycle tunnels with a larger vehicular one to follow, Minister of Transport Alfred Barnes ceremoniously cut the first turf on the Tyne's south bank at Jarrow. After years of argument,

During the 1950s and '60s, 20,000 people a day used the Tyne pedestrian and cycle tunnel. Some are pictured here on the Howdon side, with the steeple of Christ Church Jarrow prominent on the opposite bank. The two tunnels under the river were not the first. A 977-foot-long shaft, built in 1898, linked Hebburn to Wallsend. It carried power cables and later fibre-optic lines, across the Tyne. *Newcastle Evening Chronicle*.

In 2010 the tunnel entrance at Howdon is a much quieter place. Recent problems with ageing lifts and escalators have curtailed the tunnel's use, but the Tyne & Wear Integrated Transport Authority is determined to renovate them and raise their profile. Though the 'Fish Artworks' installed several years ago on the northern side might have not met with great enthusiasm, it is hoped that emphasising the tunnels' link to the National Cycle Network will be more successful. At least acknowledgement is given to George Stephenson and his son Robert, who was born nearby in 1803.

the Howdon to Jarrow tunnel route – 6 miles to the east of Newcastle – was agreed to be the best and least expensive option. It was clear that the Tyne's newest bridge, opened in 1928 between Newcastle and Gateshead, could do little to ease the strain on ferry services down stream. At times during the war, in particular, more than 7,000 passengers a day – most bound for local shipyards and factories – were ferried over the river on vessels of variable ages and conditions. But many riverside works would be within easy reach of the new tunnels, which began to be driven out from the Jarrow shore.

In keeping with its early history, however, the building of the tunnel was also protracted. After starting on the Jarrow side, boring from both banks continued round the clock to defeat a riverbed tougher than anticipated. Main contractor Charles Brand & Sons drafted in extra machinery from London, but the time taken to complete the work still exceeded all original estimates. Nevertheless – overdue and over-budget as the completed tunnels were – their technical accomplishments could not be denied.

With MP Alfred Barnes again officiating, the twin tunnels were formally opened in July 1951. At that time they were the world's longest, and each 900-foot shaft, strengthened with cast-iron linings, carried a gas main across the river. Both tunnels were fully tiled, creating acoustic effects that soon became apparent. Thousands ventured through the cool passages on that first day, reaching them by steeply inclined escalators that, after more than half a century and with few modifications, are still the longest of their kind.

Only a few years after their opening, the tunnels were prophetically deemed by some to be totally inadequate for the demands of a modern car-bound age. And although easily outstripping the Howdon ferry in passenger numbers at first, tunnel usage did fall alarmingly as the shipyards closed.

Consequently, the Tyne's first sub-river 'foot' crossing was indeed overtaken by the car and overshadowed by the road tunnel built alongside it in the 1960s. Its big brother has now been unveiled as the final component of the 'Tyne Tunnel Project'. But the first of the trio remains – still toll-free and open all hours. With its 'tiny echoing passages' and clattering wooden escalators, the Tyne pedestrian and cycle tunnels are often deserted gems. Their antiquated image may yet be raised from the hidden depths to which they have sunk.

Opposite bottom: **An Auty picture postcard immortalises the opening of the Albert Edward Dock in 1884. On a calm river at half past two in the afternoon, the steamer *Para-E-Amazonas* glides into the new dock. When the Royal vessel passed Hebburn (where it was built for a South American company), local schoolchildren waved handkerchiefs to form an outline of the Prince of Wales's feathers. Matthew Auty abandoned his trade as a tobacconist to become a photographer. As well as topical subjects, he created picturesque images that popularised the North East coast and countryside.** *Newcastle City Library*

Opposite top: **Nowadays Armstrong's accumulator tower mainly witnesses pleasure craft entering the Royal Quays. Over a working life of about a century these docks at Coble Dene were deemed to be a commercial failure. Yet 20 hydraulic and steam cranes handled countless vessels in a dock complex noteworthy for the import of timber as well as the export of coal. As part of a £230 million Royal Quays project, work began in October 1997 to revitalise the redundant Albert Edward Dock. Some of its Victorian dock gates were preserved, while others were renewed and a new control tower was built.**

40. North Shields: Albert Edward Dock

Tyneside's latest marina and shopping 'outlet' is well named. One mile from the centre of North Shields and now known popularly as the Royal Quays, it was opened as the Albert Edward Dock by the Prince of Wales in 1884. The historic

A cross-river view from the archives gives a clear view of the accumulator tower and an attendant steam engine chimney. Alongside is a low hill, formed by decades of unloaded ballast.
North Tyneside Libraries (North Shields).

former dock, originally built for vessels from the coal and timber trade, now hosts a more glamorous fleet. Yet among the modern masts and spars remains one last Victorian gem.

Shaped by streams running through the 'Coble Dene', this sandy stretch of the northern riverbank was a natural landing point long before a dock was built. Until Percy Main pit and its waggonways began to determine its future in the early 19th century, the area was used primarily for salt production. But the needs of the coal trade prevailed and calls for improved shipping facilities began to grow louder.

Church bells were rung and cannon fired to celebrate the passing of the first Tyne Improvement Act in 1850, but its early results were less spectacular. After its first decade, the Tyne Commission was attacked

The ferryboat *Spirit of the Tyne* churns upstream past Royal Quays on 24 July 2010. From this angle it appears that the accumulator tower has acquired a new companion – it is 'Tyne Anew', an art installation by Mark di Suvero. Completed in 1999, it is grandly claimed to 'conduct and point to an evolving industrial background'; locals have dubbed the spindly red structure 'the Tyne Tripod'. To its left is the *Earl of Zetland*, now a floating pub. Built at Aberdeen in 1939, she was pressed into war service, joining the legendary 'little ships' off Dunkirk in May 1940.

North Shields: Albert Edward Dock

for failing to deepen a river once condemned as a 'cursed horse pond'. Nevertheless, new docks had been constructed by the Commissioners on both banks of the river, and with the appointment of John F. Ure a man was found who would 'make' the Tyne.

Fresh from his modernisation work on the Clyde, Ure began as Tyneside's chief river engineer in December 1858. In return for his £1,000 annual salary he brought new vigour to the long-overdue task of river improvements and reversed what a leading South Shields historian of the day called the Commission's 'peddling policy'. A keen advocate of dredging, Ure drove forward his ambitious plans and ushered in an era of considerable river improvements on the Tyne.

Despite his success on Tyneside, however, Ure never lived to see the completion of his third major dock. Designs made before he retired in 1878 were left for his successor, P. J. Messent, to fully implement. After an earlier site further downstream was abandoned, work started at Coble Dene – on land bought from the Duke of Northumberland – in 1873. Legal and financial obstacles delayed it for another decade until the 24-acre dock surrounded by deep-water quays was ready for business. Built primarily for the import trade during a period of relative decline, it was none the less provided with a coal staith capable of loading the largest vessels.

On 21 August 1884 the paddle-steamer carrying Prince Albert and his wife cut through ribbons stretched across the entrance of the new dock. A banner was unfurled on the staiths and Ure's final dock scheme on Tyneside was declared open. Not surprisingly it made extensive use of Lord Armstrong's hydraulic machinery, controlled by a power system that he developed and of the type that began to appear in Britain's emergent docklands from the mid-19th century onwards. Within the accumulator's stone tower, pressurised water was held in reserve to operate a medley of dockyard equipment, from lock gates to cranes, capstans to conveyors.

Accumulator housings remain in various architectural guises around the country, but Royal Quay's example is unique on Tyneside. At the end of the 20th century, one of the Tyne & Wear Development Company's last acts was to preserve the approximately 60-foot-high structure as part of the disused dock's transformation into the 400-berth 'Harbour World Marina'. Though it may appear to be more Northumbrian Peel Tower than industrial gem, this old dock building is another reminder of the determined Victorian ingenuity that improved the Tyne and helped make our modern world.

Pictured in 2010, redundant dock machinery from the old Albert Edward Dock seems to have become an addition to the Royal Quay's modern art.

41. North Shields: Maritime Chambers

High above the Tyne at North Shields, Maritime Chambers faces the sea-lanes that played a significant part in its history. Erected in 1806, the two-storey structure at Number One Howard Street was first used as a library and lecture theatre before it embraced a seafaring role.

In the 1890s Joseph Robinson & Sons turned this sandstone-fronted building into the headquarters of its expanding shipping business. The company had been established by James Robinson, who moved from Whitby in 1796 as a ship's First Mate to further his career on Tyneside. At North Shields he discovered a riverside community attempting to break free from the centuries-old trading restrictions imposed on it by Newcastle. And indeed, from a sparsely populated 'poor and miserable place' of saltpans and fishing boats in the mid-18th century, the small harbour town was starting to grow up. Narrow stairways connected a crowded lower riverbank to elegant streets and squares on the heights 60 feet above. Some of these contained the well-appointed residences of traders, ship-owners and former mariners, already enjoying the success to which James Robinson aspired.

Opportunity eventually arose for Robinson in 1817, when falling prices after

The Stag Line building is unmistakable in this North Shields photograph. Taken prior to the waterside regeneration of the late 20th century, the image also highlights Liddell Street graving dock at the end of a long working life. Ship-repair facilities such as this were indispensable, allowing the dock to be pumped dry before 'graving' or scraping the vessel's hull clean of rust and barnacles. Built in the early 19th century, this now protected ancient monument was mainly used to build and repair fishing boats, and became known locally as the 'Haddock Shop'. *North Tyneside Libraries (North Shields)*

North Shields: Maritime Chambers

the Napoleonic Wars allowed him to buy the *Blessing*, a modest 221-ton ship, launched at Sunderland some years before. The vessel steered the young company through difficult times, surviving another economic slow-down and the death of their founder in 1833. Even losing their prized brig in 1846 proved to be something of a blessing in disguise.

With the insurance payout from *Blessing*, new owner Joseph Robinson ordered the ship that effectively created the 'Stag Line' name. Built in a South Shields yard, the *Stag* strengthened the company and launched a figurehead soon to be emblazoned on the flags and funnels of Stag Line ships. Derived from a Robinson family coat of arms, the heraldic stag 'trippant' became the distinctive emblem of its Tyneside fleet, which by 1871 comprised nine vessels, and within a decade had increased to 11 – all steam-powered.

Though at first still often backed up by sails, the steamer began to dominate the seaways as the 19th century progressed. Improvements to compound steam engines accelerated the process, but it was Tyneside's innovative *John Bowes* that pointed the way. Owned and built by the Palmer brothers at Jarrow in 1852, their twin-hulled, screw-driven collier speeded up coastal trade and pioneered a water ballast system that set the precedent for fleets of ocean-going 'tramp' steamers in the years to come.

Well into the 20th century the bulk carriers of Robinson's Stag Line (many built and maintained on the Tyne) contributed to the 'Geordie' complement of this worldwide trading fleet. Battling back after heavy wartime losses, the North Shields organisation even diversified temporarily into cable-laying. But unlike the first recession, which helped to start Stag Line, a modern shipping decline finished it off. In 1981 Tyneside's oldest independent shipping line became a subsidiary of oil and gas conglomerate Hunting PLC, and Stag's final vessel – the *Segonia* – was sold two years later.

During a rarely celebrated history, Stag Line transported almost every cargo imaginable – from coal to grain, hides to molasses – to destinations across the globe. Its former home-port offices eventually reopened as the Stag Line pub and restaurant in 1992. Somewhat marooned from the modern town, a renovated Maritime Chambers now serves as North Shields Registrars Office and a bureau for the Duke of Edinburgh Awards scheme. Its gable end still proudly displaying a large Stag crest, this dignified gem is included as a final symbol of Tyneside's long industrial story and the great river that runs through every page.

The old 'Stag' still holds its head high above a riverbank now crowded with modern buildings.

An engraving from the *Illustrated London News* shows Howard Street and Maritime Chambers when crowds were celebrating the new Borough of Tynemouth's first municipal elections on 1 November 1849. Bands played and blazing tar barrels were rolled along the street.

Now contained within luxury apartments on 'Dolphin Quays', Liddell Street's historic Low Dock is private property. But the public square outside Maritime Chambers could be no better place for a seamen's memorial. Unveiled in 1997, it features a ship's anchor and is inscribed: 'For all those lost at sea Lord grant them safe harbour'.

Index

A. & P. Tyne 33
Armstrong,
  Lord William 9, 90, 91, 105, 106-107, 136-137
Askew family 53
Associated Lead Manufacturers 90
Auty, Matthew 136
Axwell Hall 67-69

Barnes, Alfred 135-136
Barras, John & Co 111, 112
Beaumont, Huntingdon 7
Birtley 44
Blackett, Christopher 84
Blackett, John 82
Blackett, William 91
Blackham's Hill 39, 40, 41
Blaydon 73-77
Blaydon Burn 75-77, 119
Boullemier, Lucien 125
Bowes, George 67
Bowes, Sir William 64
Bowes Railway 39-41, 84
Brand, Charles & Sons 136
Brandling Junction 42-44
Brandling, William and John 11, 44
Brewing 110-111
Bridon International Ropes 134
Brigham & Cowan 16-17
Brown, Irene 17
Brown, William 82
Bruce, John 112
Buddle, John 129-130
Burns, George 74

Carr-Ellison, Ralph 35, 38
Chaldron wagons 7, 61
Chance, James 32
Chapman, William and Edward 61, 131, 133
Charleton, R. J. 9, 95, 122
Chemical industry 10, 45
Cherry, John 93
Chopwell 68-69
Clapham, Anthony 45
Clara Vale 78-81
Clavering family 67-69
Cleadon 25
Coalmining 7, 10, 39, 60-62, 79, 86, 90, 129-130
Coke production 70-72
Company of Hostmen 7
Cookson, Isaac 13
Cookson & Walker 90
Cowen, Sir Joseph 75-76
Craggs, Joseph and Robert 51
Crowley, Ambrose 7-8, 63-66, 76

Darby, Abraham 70
Davy, Humphrey 35, 129
Defoe, Daniel 6, 60
Dobson,
  John 35, 52-54, 58, 69, 114, 115-117, 120
Dodd, Ralph 135
Donnelly, Henry 115
Douglass, James 32
Dunston Staiths 60
Durham Miners Association 73

Easton, Thomas 46
Edison, Thomas Alva 57
Electrical industry 10, 118
Ellison,
  Robert, Henry and Cuthbert 38
Ellison Hall 35-36, 37

Felling 42-43, 45
Fetch, Ernest 21
Forster, Jonathon 84
Friar's Goose colliery 45-46, 130

Gateshead 8, 44, 45, 50-51, 67
  Baltic Centre 108
  Bensham 52-54
  Central Hotel 47
  Greenesfield Works 48-49
  Kells Lane 55
  Low Fell 55-57
  Pipewellgate 47-48
  Sage Concert Hall 108
  Team Valley Trading Estate 127
  Windmill Hills 51

Gateshead & District
  Tramways 52, 54
Gilhespie, W. 93
Gillott & Johnson 129
Glass manufacturing 13, 15, 88-89
Gosforth colliery 10
Grace, William 63
Grain milling 75-77
Grainger, Richard 92-93, 94, 115
'Grand Allies' 40-41
Green, John and Benjamin 131

Hackworth, Timothy 8, 84
Harrison, T. E. 106-107
Harton 12, 13
Hawks, Crawshay & Sons 50
Hawks, George 50
Hawks, William 7-8
Hawksley, Thomas 25-27
Hawthorn, R. & W./Hawthorn Leslie 33
Heaton 126-128

Hebburn 33-38
Hedley, William 8, 84, 122
Hepburn, Thomas 73
Hockin, Cecil 127
Hodgson, Richard 38
Holmes, Frederick Hale 31-32
Hood, R., Haggie & Son 131, 133
Hoults,
  removals and storage 124, 126
Howdon Pedestrian Tunnel 135-135
Hudson, George 44, 49
Hunting PLC 143
Hurst, Richard 65
Hutt, William 51

Iron and steelmaking 86

Johnson, R. J. 85

Keelboats 7, 120-121
Keelmen 6, 120-122
Kell, William 55
Killingworth colliery 98

Lamb, Joseph 89
Leadmaking 90-91
Lemington glassworks 4, 88-89
Leslie, Andrew 33-34, 36
Liddell family 58-59, 69
Lime production 28-30
Longridge, Michael 98
Losh, William 8
Lovibond, Thomas 112

McClellan 119
Macklin, Thomas Eyre 111
'Main Dike Stone' 10
Maling Pottery 123-126
Mansell, Sir Robert 88
Marsden 28-32
Marshall family 23
Mather, James 12
Mawson, John 55
Merz, Charles 119
Merz, Theodore 57
Messent, Phillip J. 106, 139
Metro, Tyneside 43, 101, 134
Mill Dam glassworks 12-13
Mount Moor colliery 40, 41
Mylne, Robert 105

Newburn 85-87

Newcastle-upon-Tyne
  Bath Lane 112, 113
  Carliol House 118-119
  'Chimney Mill' 95-97
  Claremont Road 93, 95, 96, 97

Elswick 90, 105
Forth Banks 98, 104
Glasshouse Bridge 125
Hanover Street 101-104
Haymarket 111, 113
High Level Bridge 50, 106-7
Keelman's Hospital 120-122
King Edward VII Bridge 101
Lying-In Hospital 115-116
Millennium Bridge 105, 108, 121
Mosley Street 57, 118
New Bridge Street 115-117
Newcastle Brewery 110-114
Ouseburn 9, 88, 123-126
Percy Street 112, 113
Queen Elizabeth II
    Metro Bridge 101
Royal Jubilee School 120
St Thomas Street 113, 114
Sandgate 120-122
South Street
    Locomotive Works 98-100
Spital Tongues 93, 94, 95, 97
Swing Bridge 104, 105-109, 122
Tyne Road bridge 108
Victoria Tunnel 92-94

Newcastle & North Shields
    Railway 134
Newcastle Electric
    Supply Co 118-119
Nixon, David 94
North Eastern Railway 48, 62, 98

North Shields 16, 135
    Albert Edward Dock 136-139
    Coble Dene 138, 139
    Howard Street 142
    Maritime Chambers 140-143
    Royal Quays 137, 139

North Wylam 82
Northumberland, Dukes of 85, 87, 88, 122, 139
Northumberland Glass Co 88
Northumberland Paper Mills 63

Oakwellgate 44

Paine, James 58, 67
Palmer, Charles 9, 112, 141
Parsons, Charles 118
Path Head watermill, Blaydon 75-77

Pease, Edward 98
Porter & Latimer 93
Potts, John Cuthbert 47
Pride of the Tyne, ferry 14

Rainhill trials 99
Ramsey, Thomas 73-74
Ravensworth Castle 58-59
Ravensworth, Lord 69
Readhead, James 23
Redheugh 7, 44, 51, 53
Reed, Charles 112
Richardson, Thomas 98
Robert Stephenson & Hawthorns
    Ltd 98, 100
Robinson, Joseph & Sons 140-141
Rowlands Gill 70
Russell, William 129

St Hilda's colliery 11-12
Salt production 8
Sanderson, John & Sons 113
Scotswood, Newburn & Wylam
    Railway 82
Scottish & Newcastle 113
Shipbuilding and repairing 9, 16
Smeaton, John 96-97
Souter Point Lighthouse 31-32

South Shields 6, 11ff, 28, 30, 44, 135
    Alum Ale House 14-15
    Market Dock 16-17
    Town Halls 18-21

Sowerby family 89
Spencer, John 86
Spirit of the Tyne, ferry 14, 138
Spoor, Amor 101, 103
Springwell 39-41
Stag Line 16, 140-141, 143
Stanhope & Tyne Railway 44
Steam engines 8, 25, 41, 45-46
    Boulton & Watt 46
    Newcomen 8, 46
    Trevithick 47
Stella colliery 68, 78-80
Stella Hall 75, 76
Stephenson,
    George 8, 40, 47, 82-84, 86, 98-100, 129, 131, 135
Stephenson,
    Robert 98-100, 106-107, 112, 131, 135

Stephenson Clarke Line 61
Stevenson, James Cochran 23, 57
Stockton & Darlington
    Railway 40, 42, 98, 99
Stokoe, John 115
Sunderland &
    South Shields Water Co 25
Swalwell and ironworks 63, 68, 97
Swan, Joseph Wilson 55-57, 118
Swan Hunter & Wigham
    Richardson 128
Swinburne, Robert 13

Taylor, Hugh 85, 87
Tempest family 76
Temple, Simon 16
Templetown 11
Thompson, George 80
Thompson, Matthew 47
Tide stone, Newburn 87
Trevithick, Richard 47, 84
Tyne & Wear Industrial
    Monuments Trust 71, 72
Tyne ferries 14
Tyne Improvement Commission 32, 106, 109, 121

Ure, John F. 106, 139

Vale Mill Trust 77

Waggonways 7, 60, 82-84
Walkers, Fishwick & Co 91
Wallsend 128-130
Water supplies 25
Watts, William 91
Wesley, John 120
Westoe and its Hall 12, 22-24
Whinfield 70-72
Whinfield, John 47
Whitburn 12, 28, 29, 30
Willington, ropery
    and viaduct 131-134
Wills cigarette factory 126-128
Winlaton 7, 64-66
Wylam 82